LIFE LESSONS

Shaun Attwood

My Social-Media Links

Email: attwood.shaun@hotmail.co.uk
Blog: Jon's Jail Journal
Website: shaunattwood.com
Twitter: @shaunattwood
YouTube: Shaun Attwood
LinkedIn: Shaun Attwood
Goodreads: Shaun Attwood
Facebook pages: Shaun Attwood, Jon's Jail Journal,
T-Bone Appreciation Society

I welcome feedback on any of my books.
Thank you for the Amazon reviews!

Shaun's Books

English Shaun Trilogy
Party Time
Hard Time
Prison Time

War on Drugs Series
Pablo Escobar: Beyond Narcos
American Made: Who Killed Barry Seal?
Pablo Escobar or George HW Bush
The Cali Cartel: Beyond Narcos
We Are Being Lied To: The War on Drugs (Expected 2019)
The War Against Weed (Expected 2019)

Un-Making a Murderer:
The Framing of Steven Avery and Brendan Dassey
The Mafia Philosopher: Two Tonys
Life Lessons

Pablo Escobar's Story (Expected 2018)
T-Bone (Expected 2022)

Contents

Contents

Introduction

Bang, bang, bang, bang, bang!

**"Tempe Police Department!
We have a warrant!"**

I leap up from my computer table. My insides clench. I rush to the door. The peephole's blacked out. Feeling the threat from the other side, I flinch back. Through a window, I see police positioned behind cars and marksmen aiming rifles. Afraid of getting shot, I duck. *Get the hell out!* Blood surges to my head. *Hide in the ceiling? Jump off the balcony? Nowhere to go! I'm trapped!*

I'm halfway through the living room when – *boom!* – the door leaps off its hinges. Pointing huge guns, the SWAT team barricades me in with a wall of Plexiglas shields. Fear of getting shot paralyses me. My chest seizes up. *The price has finally come for all of my wrongdoing.*

"Get on the ground now!"

For committing numerous drug-related crimes over the years, I end up in the jail with the highest death rate

1

in America, where gang members and even guards are murdering inmates, the food is a mystery-meat slop that sometimes has dead rats in it, and cockroaches tickle my limbs and try to crawl in my ears at night. The prosecutor labels me a drug lord, but as I stare at the blood-splattered cement-block wall in my cell it dawns on me that the only thing I'm the lord over is my own demise.

Looking back, I credit incarceration for saving my life. Before my arrest, my drug-crazed behaviour was so extreme, I once smashed my head through a plasterboard wall, just missing a lengthy nail by a few inches. I woke up caked in vomit and with no memory of it at all. The carpet cleaner couldn't remove the stains due to the toxicity of the chemicals I'd puked. My biggest competitor in the Ecstasy market, the Mafia mass murderer "Sammy the Bull" Gravano had a hit team searching for me headed by his son, and I was under the protection of the New Mexican Mafia, the most dangerous criminal organization in Arizona.

Incarcerated, wondering how on earth I was still alive, I went on an amazing journey of self-discovery. Previously, having worked my way up from a penniless student to a stock-market millionaire and Ecstasy dealer, I'd rushed through life without any introspection. Getting pushed to the brink of suicidal madness while facing a maximum 200-year sentence changed the way I think. The intense suffering I brought on myself instilled me with an appreciation of the pain of others and the urge to help them. It opened my eyes to the value of small things. I saw how emotionally immature, selfish and foolish my behaviour had been. The pain I caused my family made both them and myself ill, but added extra motivation to my soul-searching. I regretted sending people down the road of drug use, which devastates so many.

Shocked, ashamed, I set out to try and make sense of my behaviour in the hope of becoming a better person. I read over 1000 books, and submerged myself in psychology, philosophy, yoga and meditation. I was fortunate enough to have counselling with a brilliant psychotherapist, Dr. Owen, and to be guided by Two Tonys, a Mafia mass murderer who left a trail made up of the corpses of rival gangsters that stretched from Tucson to Alaska. After I started putting his stories on the Internet, Two Tonys, a self-taught philosopher serving over 100 years, took me under his wing. To this day, I fall back on what I learned while incarcerated and what others, including my meditation teacher, Andrew, continue to teach me.

Since my release six years ago, I've been blessed to share my experiences as a motivational speaker with tens of thousands of students. My jail activism was featured in an episode of *Banged-Up Abroad* televised worldwide on National Geographic Channel, and my story was published as a trilogy. But just as importantly, I wake up with a smile on my face because I feel at peace with myself and the world. In this book, I'm going to share the lessons I learned that transformed my life.

Lesson 1:
Make Slow and
Careful Progress

"Make haste slowly."
– Gaius Suetonius Tranquillus

At age 14, I set myself the goal of becoming a millionaire. In high school, I show an aptitude for Economics, so the teacher takes me under his wing. He gives me extra lessons on my own and explains how to understand the stock market. When I'm 16, I grow excited about TV commercials advertising the privatisation of British Telecom. The UK government is offering shares at 50p and I can smell money-making potential. After discussing the prospects with my teacher, I borrow £50 from my grandmother to invest. On the first day of dealings, BT shares double. I dance around the house yelling, "Yes! Yes! Yes!" I take an immediate profit. Hooked on the stock market, I invest in every privatization I can get my hands on. Each privatization is oversubscribed (meaning that more investors applied for shares than are being offered). To ensure that I get plenty of shares, I submit applications in all of my family members' names. I order dozens of books on the stock market from the library – with topics ranging from number crunching to crowd psychology – which I devour with fanaticism.

After graduating from The University of Liverpool with a BA in Business Studies, I leave my small industrial hometown in Northwest England for Phoenix, Arizona in May 1991. All I have to survive on are my student credit cards and an unshakeable belief that conquering the stock market is my destiny. I aim to get rich by using the skills I've acquired from studying and trading the stock market, and by applying my two favourite mottos:

"Greed is good." – Gordon Gekko in *Wall Street*

**"It's dog eat dog in the business world."
– My aunt Mo whom I idolize**

I fib to the immigration official at the airport that I'm only in America for a brief holiday to visit my Aunt Mo who'd settled in Arizona with her husband. I illegally apply for employment by mailing my résumé to all of the stockbrokerages listed in the phone book. Days later at Aunt Mo's house, I receive a letter from a brokerage offering a job interview. As I don't have a Social Security card that's valid for employment, I seek Aunt Mo's advice. She says to tell the brokerage that she keeps all of my important documents in her safe, and I'd be happy to bring them a photocopy. She shows me how to forge an H-1B professional-level job visa using a simple printing set from a stationery store.

At the interview, I'm offered a job on the spot. It's commission only, so I won't make any money until I start opening new accounts. I also have to obtain a Series 7 stock-brokerage license, which involves attending two months of classes, during which time I won't get paid. Worried about running out of credit, I convince the branch manager that I don't need the classes because of my education and stock-market experience. Two weeks later, I ace the Series 7 exam, igniting a sense of invincibility within me.

In the cutthroat world of rookie stockbroking, I must attend a 6am sales meeting and cold-call 500 numbers daily to build a pipeline of leads of potential investors. My first few months, I open no new accounts. Running out of credit, I'm reduced to living off cheese sandwiches and bananas. In the hope of increasing my chances of success, I enter a business partnership with another rookie, Matt. We pledge to watch each other's backs.

Exhausted from months of relentless cold-calling, I suggest to Matt that we try dumpster-diving other broker-ages for sales leads. He dismisses the idea as insane until I stick my hand in our trash and extract paperwork with our clients' names, addresses and telephone numbers.

We buy garbage gloves, trash bags and box cutters. We target a rival firm because two of their brokers recently threatened to blow up Matt's car over a mutual client. Matt drives us to the brokerage. The dumpster is enclosed by three walls and a gate at the front. We grab bags and slice them open. Eventually we find stacks of account paperwork, which we load into Matt's car. Dumpster-diving boosts my commission. Now that I'm producing results, the branch manager starts cutting me in on the distributions of accounts from brokers who periodically quit the business. That's how I rise up the ranks in my first two years.

Following a dumpster-diving mission, I'm pulled over by the police. They approach my car and shine their flashlights on the bags of trash. As they search through the bags, I fear I'm going to be arrested for industrial espionage. After they let me go with just a speeding ticket, I quit dumpster-diving.

My business partner, Matt, becomes addicted to crystal meth and loses his job, fiancée and health. Having run up a drug debt with the wrong people, he flees Arizona. I never hear from him again. Working long hours solo for two years, I get burnt out. Ignoring what happened to Matt, I start taking crystal meth to boost my energy and enhance my work performance. I tell myself, *I'll just take it a few times and never get addicted.* On the drug, I don't need any sleep. I feel super human. My telephone aggression surges. Finally, at 27-years old, I become the top producer in the office, grossing over $500,000 a year. The result is the culmination of 13 years of staying focussed on finance, but now I'm accelerating progress at all costs, unable to foresee the consequences.

Working at such a frantic pace, I need to let off steam on the weekends. I return to raving and taking Ecstasy, a habit that was my religion back in the UK during my student days. Having more money than common sense, I buy pills for all of my friends. Hanging out in the rave community, I see the business potential of throwing parties and selling Ecstasy. I decide to try a business experiment by purchasing bulk Ecstasy in LA and selling it to ravers in Phoenix.

Two carloads of us, including my big best friend from childhood, Wild Man, drive to an Ecstasy dealer's house in West Hollywood. He isn't home, so we sit for a few hours, fretting over whether we're being set up or the police will eventually notice us parked there. My stress is peaking when the dealer finally arrives. Wild Man offers to beat him up and rob the Ecstasy as punishment for him keeping us waiting. "That's not good business," I say, and ask Wild Man to stay put for now, but to come and rescue me if I'm not out in fifteen minutes.

Walking to the house, I'm terrified of getting robbed at gunpoint, or kidnapped and held for ransom, or even shot. I fear the police may have the place under surveillance and maybe they'll pull me over when I have the drugs in my car or track me all of the way back to Phoenix and arrest me there. I'm concerned about buying pills that are cut with something other than Ecstasy. Entering the house, not knowing what I'm getting into, I brace for someone to jump out and stick a gun in my face. I relax when I see a bag of pills with the Mitsubishi logo on them. As I'm familiar with the taste of Ecstasy, I insist on chewing one to avoid buying junk. It tastes right, so I leave satisfied, but wary of getting intercepted by the police on the journey home.

In Tempe, I host a party at Wild Man's apartment. Over the weekend, the 500 pills sell fast. I get lavished with so much attention, I feel like a rock star. I also make $5000 in profit. The experiment has succeeded. *Imagine how much money you could make if you apply your business knowledge to selling Ecstasy and how much fun you could have.* High on drugs and the buzz of the party lifestyle, I think that quitting my job as a stockbroker to sell Ecstasy is a brilliant idea.

In 1999, with hundreds of people working for me, I become the biggest Ecstasy dealer in Arizona – until Sammy the Bull Gravano sets up an Ecstasy ring in competition with mine. A former underboss of the Gambino Crime Family under Teflon Don John Gotti, The Bull confessed to committing 19 Mafia-related murders. He was relocated to Tempe, Arizona as part of the US Federal Witness Protection Program. After The Bull's thugs knock the teeth out of my top Ecstasy salesperson and offer a reward to anyone who can lead them to me, I flee to Tucson. I move into a million-dollar mountainside home in a gated guarded community, where I feel safer.

Hoping to have a peaceful night out in the last place my rivals would try to find me, I go to a gay club called The Crow Bar in downtown Phoenix. High on Ecstasy and relaxing with my friends, I'm soon enjoying the friendly atmosphere and the house music pumping from giant black speakers. The floor is packed with topless muscular men, some in yellow construction hats, dancing under flickering strobe lights. I dare any of my friends to dance topless with a construction hat. With a massive Ecstasy grin, Wild Man gets on the floor and shakes his stuff surrounded by hip-grinding hunks.

A strip-tease dancer partying in the Crow Bar recognizes me and calls Sammy the Bull's crew – which I'm unaware of until Sammy the Bull's son tells me in prison years later. The Bull dispatches his son as the head of an armed team with instructions to kidnap me from the Crow Bar. They're going to hold me for ransom, and if the ransom isn't paid, they're going to take me out to the desert and kill me to eliminate their competition. Fortunately, Wild Man gets in a scuffle and we have to leave the Crow Bar in a hurry. The Gravano crew arrive too late.

In February 2000, the police wipe out my competition by arresting Sammy the Bull, his wife, daughter, son and 31 co-defendants. With them in jail, I assume the investigation of the rave scene will wind down, but the number of undercover agents increases. I decide to quit Ecstasy dealing and resume trading the stock market, but it's too late. On May 16th 2002, the SWAT team smashes my door down.

To realize my dream of becoming a millionaire, I set out on the sure path of hard and conscientious work. But as I became more successful, my psychology altered until I no longer viewed the law as an obstacle. Every time I cut a corner and got away with it, my sense of invincibility grew. Over time, the magnitude of my law-breaking, drug consumption and Ecstasy dealing increased until I lost sight of why I was in America. Due to my bad choices, everything I ever earned, including my stockbroker's pension, was confiscated by the State of Arizona. I wouldn't have lost everything, including almost six years of my life, if I had maintained slow and careful progress instead of being side-tracked by the thrill of the party scene.

Reflecting on that lesson in prison, I swear never to repeat those mistakes. In 2004 when I'm starting to serve the balance of my sentence in a so-called supermax (or super-maximum security) prison in Florence, Arizona, the BBC runs a story about my jail blog and activism. The media attention produces positive feedback on my writing. I set a goal of becoming an author. With no English education beyond high school, I know it won't be easy for a convicted Ecstasy dealer to get published. But I'm also driven by the belief that success is a function of effort and perseverance. There'll be no cutting corners this time.

One of the difficulties of getting published is finding a literary agent. An agent is considered harder to get than a publisher, and most serious publishers won't read a manuscript unless the author has a reputable agent. Luckily, an agent who's read my blog contacts me, expressing interest in a potential autobiography. But as I'm clueless about the profession, I quickly burn that bridge by writing poorly and failing to understand her guidance. The agent tells my family that I'll never be an author – which disappoints me at first, but later inspires me to try harder.

Learning the lingo of the literary profession is as difficult as studying a foreign language. In prison, I spend all day reading and writing, honing my skills. I'm told reading will improve my writing, so I set a goal of reading over 1000 books by my release, which I achieve in just under six years. Upon my release in December 2007, I set a goal of getting my story published within five years. By maintaining the work ethic I'd adhered to in prison, I manage to get the first instalment of the English Shaun trilogy, *Hard Time*, published in 2010. Book sales don't come easy for an unpublished unknown ex-con. At my first book signing, only two people show up – and they've come to see the other author signing that day. I do manage to sell one copy to someone who feels sorry for me: the partner of the other author. Again, I know that perseverance is the key. Together with my mum – who quickly becomes my top salesperson – I recruit a team of helpers and dress them in the black-and-white bee stripes I wore in the Maricopa County jail. Within two years, I become the top selling local author at Waterstones, the biggest chain of bookstores in the UK, selling 100 to 150 copies at each signing. The majority of my sales now are Internet based and managing my social media is a full-time job.

The road to fast cash is full of danger. If I had remained satisfied with slow and steady progress as a stockbroker, I'd have gone on to higher success. I'd probably be worth about $10 million by now and not be banned from America for life. By taking my time and persevering in the face of numerous setbacks in the last decade, I've rebuilt my life on a solid platform. Knowing that it can't be pulled from under my feet gives me a sense of peace and security. The success

I've achieved so far has opened doors into other areas such as writing this book. The whole new positive direction my life is going in is a key ingredient in my happiness and it's a credit to slow and careful progress.

Lesson 2: Help Others

"Those who are happiest are those
who do the most for others."
– Booker T. Washington

"Lockdown, everybody!" a guard announces at 8pm in the maximum-security Madison Street jail in May 2003.

We trudge back to our tiny two-man cells, slam our doors and rest on our bunks. A burly redneck guard enters our cell to perform a headcount. As part of a security procedure to check if an escape is in progress, he bangs a cane against the vent, the cement-block walls and a tiny bulletproof window caked in filth.

Just before lights out at 10pm, movement starts at the cracks in the decrepit walls, accompanied by rustling. American cockroaches the size of almonds are lining up like an army waiting to invade, shuffling against each other in the competition for space, with their long antennae protruding. They move ever so slightly back and forth as if they can barely wait. As soon as a guard hits the light switch, they flood the room. Every now and then, one drops from the ceiling and resumes crawling on the grimy cement floor. Having arrived before me, my cellmate wisely chose the top bunk to avoid the cockroaches pouring from the gaps around my bunk brackets, inches away from where I sleep. Walking to the toilet, I crunch a few cockroaches under my shower sandals. When I grab the toilet roll, a cockroach darts from it onto my hand, tickling my fingers. My arm jerks, losing both the cockroach and toilet roll.

Nauseous, I sit on a stool, wondering how on earth I'm going to get to sleep, disgusted yet in awe of how alive the walls look. Tired of flicking them off my feet, I cocoon myself in a sheet and lay down sideways on my bunk, crushing a few cockroaches. The only way they can crawl on me now is by entering a breathing hole I've left in the sheet. Inhaling their musty odour, I close my eyes, but I can't sleep. Listening to the swamp-cooler vent – a metal grid at the top of a wall – hissing out tepid air, I feel cockroaches moving on the sheet around my feet. *Am I imagining things?* My eyes keep opening to see if they've infiltrated my breathing hole. With my body cramping, I rotate onto my other side. Facing the wall, I'm repulsed by the cockroaches zigging and zagging just inches away. I return to my original side. The sheet traps the heat of the Sonoran Desert to my body, coating me in sweat, aggravating my bleeding and itching skin infections and bedsores, some of which look as if I've spilt battery acid on myself. The ticklish sweat tricks my mind into thinking that the cockroaches are on me. I want to scratch myself, but I know better. From sweating constantly, the outer layers of my skin have turned soggy. Squirming on the bunk fails to stop the relentless itchiness of my skin. Eventually, I succumb to scratching myself. Clumps of moist skin detach under my nails. The heat trapped by the sheet is unbearable. I discard the sheet, resigned to offering my body to the cockroaches. They start out tickling my feet, limbs, palms…

Having not slept properly since my arrival in the cell several days ago, I start hallucinating and hearing voices whispering threats. Facing a maximum 200-year sentence, I'm at breaking point. Although I committed crimes and deserve to be punished, no one should have to live like this. I'm furious at myself for making the series of reckless decisions that put me in here and for losing absolutely everything. I remember what my life used to be like.

At the peak of my Ecstasy business, a typical day involved rising around noon in a million-dollar mountainside home in Tucson. When it rained, a beautiful waterfall would form behind the house and a stream would gargle past our little wooden gate. With the sun high in a usually cloudless sky above the desert, I would wake myself up by jumping in the pool with my now ex-wife, Amy. After swimming, we'd head to our favourite Indian restaurant – where I once accidentally left $30,000 in drug money in a manila envelope, and the owner found it, contacted me and returned it. Later on, my right-hand man, Cody, would arrive to discuss my illegal business, including who needed more Ecstasy, who was having problems paying for drugs, and how much cash he'd collected and secured in an apartment I rented for that purpose. Hoping to avoid police detection, we only discussed these things in person. If everything was running smoothly, I'd splurge at a fancy restaurant with Amy, take drugs and have sex. If problems arose or key business associates such as the New Mexican Mafia wanted a face-to-face meeting, I'd head to Phoenix, pick up my two toughest friends, Wild Man and G Dog, and try to fix things.

How powerful I felt strutting around with those two. And just look at me now. Reduced to nothing. Maybe never getting out of prison. Do I really want to spend the rest of my life in this kind of environment? Hell, no!

I think about taking a razor blade to my wrists and bleeding out. The thought gives me an unexpected sense of comfort. I now have a choice. *I'll wait till a guard does a security walk, slash my wrists nice and deep and just lie here with the cockroaches. The guards won't notice until the blood starts spilling from the bunk and by then it'll be too late. I wonder how long I'll take to die.*

Before committing suicide, I want to say goodbye to my family by taking a last look at their photographs. I grab an envelope containing the maximum seven pictures permitted in my personal property. I stare at the caring and loving faces of my mum, dad, sister and the fiancée who talked me into quitting the Ecstasy business. Tears pool and spill and streak down my cheeks. I close my eyes and see my mum weeping at my funeral. *She's going to get a call saying her son's slashed his wrists in an Arizona jail cell. I can't put my family through that.* Shivering and sobbing as silently as possible on my bunk, I hate myself for lacking the courage to end my life – unaware that it takes more courage to carry on. The next morning after a few hours of troubled sleep, I wake up to find the majority of the cockroaches gone for the day.

In maximum-security, most of my neighbours are facing life sentences. A gaunt freckly redhead called South Carolina limps into my cell. I ask him what's wrong. He says he has a year to live because of stomach cancer. He has syphilis, hepatitis C and herpes. Urinating is agony, and he hasn't passed a solid stool in three years. The metal screws in the steel rod in his leg have unloosened, causing constant pain. I ask him what he's in for. He says he took a foot-long knife to the woman who gave him syphilis, repeatedly stabbing her in the stomach. Facing a life sentence for attempted murder, he's going to die in here. Hearing his story, I realize things aren't so bad for me. I regret wanting to end my life.

I complain about the cockroaches to an asthmatic neighbour, middle-aged with a shaved head and tattoos from the neck down. He happily describes how he woke up breathless one morning, grabbed his inhaler and took a blast. A cockroach must have crept into the inhaler during the night because he fired the insect down his throat. Feeling it move around, he vomited, but the cockroach wasn't ejected. It remained stuck. After supressing my gag reflex, I join in with his laughter.

My cellmate, Joe, a crystal-meth chemist, is facing 20 years, but radiates inner peace. He has long brown hair, kind hazel eyes and a missing front tooth. I marvel at his happy disposition in the face of such a big sentence. A convert to the Sikh religion, he explains that it's up to us to put happiness into our lives and the lives of others, no matter how bad the jail conditions are. Joe always allows time for inmates to unload their grievances on him, no matter how petty. Even though our belongings are meagre, Joe is constantly coming up with novel ways of giving people little gifts. One of his favourite sayings is, "Giving is good." He's in pain and at risk of death, but doesn't show it. He has an inguinal hernia extending into his scrotum, trapping fluid in his scrotal pouch, which bloats like a grapefruit, causing him to urinate frequently. Even though an inmate died in the past year from a strangulated hernia, the jail refused Joe's request for an operation. Joe meditates, so whenever things deteriorate, he smiles at me, insists we place our hands in the prayer position and chant a long Aum together that usually reduces us to giggling like children. He describes every new crisis as "good suffering," which is necessary for our learning. Although his philosophy is alien to my belief system, it's working so effectively for him that I start to adopt it. Whenever I'm struggling to spend time with certain inmates who I fear or dislike, Joe insists

I especially make time for them, and jokes that it's "good giving."

A Lindo Park Crip gang member facing the death penalty for murdering several people, including shooting a woman in the face who was holding her baby up as a protective shield, walks into the cell while I'm belly-down doing a yoga position called boat and says, "You look like one of my victims trying to crawl away." I'm seized by fear. Anxiety bursts out from my solar plexus. Tongue-tied, I don't know what to say. Afterwards, I tell Joe who responds nonchalantly, "He's all right when he's not murdering people. I get along good with him." Joe's answer enables me to talk to the Lindo Park Crip without hyperventilating, and he actually takes a liking to me.

The extent of my neighbours' problems puts mine into perspective. Throughout my life, I only cared for myself and a close circle of friends, often neglecting my family. I realize that must change. In the spirit of Joe, I aim to make the most of the situation and put a little meaning and humour into our lives. I start a competition called "sufferer of the week." I offer a Snickers to the winner as voted by the rest of the prisoners. As we barely get fed, a Snickers is equivalent to a meal in here. Joe contributes a honey bun, and the competition takes off, delighting my neighbours. An early winner is a prisoner bitten by a spider. Every day he begs the guards to take him to Medical, but they decline, informing him that it's the policy of the jail not to treat insect bites. Over time, his pus-filled thumb turns fungal and black. By the time it's so bad they actually take him to Medical, he's rushed to hospital to have the thumb amputated. He says it was all worth it to get the Snickers.

Many of the prisoners can't read or write, never mind comprehend the legal terminology on their case paperwork. I start reading their cases and interpreting the jargon for them. After it becomes common knowledge that I have a book containing the Myers-Briggs personality test, about a dozen prisoners demand to be tested and ranked by me. Heated arguments ensue over who goes first. The prisoners delight in the results, flaunt them to each other and tell their family members.

Many of the Mexicans can't read or write in Spanish. No education is offered to them by the jail. Aware that I studied some basic Spanish, they ask me to start a class for them in a cell, so they can learn to write home to their loved ones. I end up with five students: four murderers, including a muscle-bound midget, and one charged with attempted murder. Mid-class, the midget, with a thick beard and a boyish happy face, usually stands, flexes his muscles like a strongman and laughs. But the murderous Aryan Brotherhood prison gang disapproves of me helping another race. Terrified, I tell Joe, who intervenes and I'm allowed to continue.

Towards the end of my two years in the jail, after seeing everything from dead rats in the chow to people getting murdered by gang members, I no longer recognize my former selfish self. I'm wracking my brains for something with more impact than "sufferer of the week." *If I can somehow draw media attention to the jail conditions things might improve for those stuck in here after I'm gone.* Adding further motivation, a guard tells me, "The world has no idea what's really going on in here," referring to the human rights violations. Around this time, my dad reads *The Clandestine Diary of an Ordinary Iraqi* by Salam Pax, which contains the blog entries Pax wrote as the bombs rained down on Baghdad. With Pax making headline news, the potential of a blog to expose the illegal conditions becomes apparent. Having seen news reports about Sheriff Joe Arpaio's guards murdering mentally-ill inmates such as Charles Agster,

Scott Norberg, and the legally blind Brian Crenshaw, my mum is worried about reprisals. After debating the safety, we decide to set the blog up under a fake name: Jon's Jail Journal.

Using a tiny pencil sharpened on the cell door, I write on sweat-soaked scraps of paper. The riskiest part is getting the writing out of the jail. I can't put it in the mail because the guards can open and inspect it for contraband. I recruit my aunt Mo. She visits me on the weekends. The visits are through Plexiglas windows with my aunt on one side and me on the other, chained to a table and speaking through a phone, so I can't hand my writing to her. I'm allowed to release property to her such as paperwork, letters and books. I hide my writing in old letters in manila envelopes and book bindings. The first time I take the property concealing my blog entries to Visitation my heart palpitates as I hand the stuff over for the guard to inspect. He searches, but as he's trained to look for contraband – drugs, syringes, cash – he doesn't notice my writing. He places my property on his table for the duration of the 30-minute visit. Talking to my aunt, I watch the guard out of the corner of my eye, convinced he's going to look through my property and find what I wrote. But he doesn't. At the end of the visit, he hands it to my aunt. I return to my cell, breathing easier, smiling as I imagine my aunt exiting the building with the blog entries. She gets home safely, types them up and emails them to my parents who post them to the Internet.

Months later, when I'm in a supermax prison, the BBC reports on Jon's Jail Journal. The blog attracts international media attention, and the number of hits snowballs. The maximum-security Madison Street jail is closed down two years after the blog started, but Sheriff Joe Arpaio runs six different jails. In 2008, a federal judge rules that the conditions in Sheriff Joe Arpaio's jail system are unconstitutional. Publicity reaches an all-time high almost a decade later when *Banged-Up Abroad* features my activism. The episode, *Raving Arizona*, is broadcast worldwide to tens of millions of viewers by National Geographic channel.

The activism leads to me becoming an author, which gives me the credibility to do talks in schools and help young people. In the cockroach-infested jail, it was beyond my imagination that I'd ever be sharing stories about the conditions in the hope of steering young people away from drugs and crime. I receive constant feedback from students such as these Tweets:

ZoeDuffy @ZoeDuffy_514 9 Aug

@shaunattwood i learnt how you just have to be careful in life even if you have made a success don't let it get to your head. Thank you

Sophie van @soph_van 8 Aug

@shaunattwood i loved it, you've put me off dealing drugs forevaa

Emma☀ @Emma_Higg 3 Aug

@shaunattwood @amycb_ don't get involved in any drug business because of the awful consequences especially in the rough American prisons

Jake McCarthy @jakepmccarthy 28 Jun

Absolutely brilliant talk from @shaunattwood yesterday, definitely the most engaging, eye opening and memorable of the week. #lessonlearned

Kieran D @KieranD 27 Jun

Great talk at school from @shaunattwood earlier. I'll

definitely make a note of the overall message: don't make terrible, terrible decisions

Tessa @TD_Tesssaa 27 Jun

Thank you @shaunattwood for talk at herts and Essex today, most interesting talk I've ever listened to, amazing

tasha @tashasaxby 27 Jun

Every teenager in the country needs to hear @shaunattwood 's speech about his prison experiences. Hits you hard.

I also receive emails from students' parents like this:

Hello Shaun,

I felt compelled to write this email as you visited my daughter's school today, Stoke Newington High, and gave a talk about the tough challenges you have been through.

Taila is my daughter who you met today and signed a book for (that she has not put down since being at home) and let me tell you how much you have touched and inspired her to the point when she rang me at work. I too was close to tears with the stories she was telling me. Never before after hearing any speaker has she come home with so much passion and emotion not forgetting interest, and I just wanted to say thank you.

Before today, I had never heard of your talk, but let me say that you will now be someone that I will never forget as I truly believe you have had that much of an impact on my daughter from just spending an afternoon with her.

It's so important for young kids to realise that all that glitters is not gold and that there are so many different ways to make in life and it all doesn't have to be materialistic.

As I read Wikipedia about you my heart races and my emotions too are running high, the pain you and your family have been through is unimaginable, and I'm just so glad you have made it through the other side not totally unscarred but a better person for it.

Having been through mentally scarring situations myself, I know the difficulties psychologically you will probably have to deal with for the rest of your life, and to think bearing that in mind you still have time to share your experiences with others.

Another interesting point Taila mentioned was that speakers have been in before telling kids don't take drugs, stay in school etc. etc. but she said you didn't preach, you just spoke about your life, and that she said was enough. What can I say but I wish you the very best for the future and hope to meet you one day.

Kind Regards,
Amanda Thompson

Reading these messages warms my heart and motivates me to keep sharing my story. People point out that the passion for what I'm doing is reflected in the tone of my voice and the shine in my eyes. Helping people keeps us focussed on the needs of others instead of our own selfish wants and desires. It acts as an automatic braking system on the ego – which when unbridled led to many of the disastrous choices I made.

Lesson 3:
Value Your Family

*"Smile at each other, make time for
each other in your family."*
– Mother Teresa

In 1996, I start buying thousands of pills of Ecstasy from LA. My parents fly from the UK to Phoenix to visit me. We're all sat comfortably in the living room of my home one evening, watching an action movie, when there's an aggressive knock on the front door. I pause the video and walk to the door. Through the peephole I see unfamiliar hostile faces. *What the hell's going on?* The second knock breaks me out in a cold sweat.

Hoping to shield my parents from what's about to unfold, I turn to them. "It's okay. I'm going to have to talk to these people. Keep the movie going." *If I answer the door with my shotgun maybe they'll be intimidated and back off.* After my parents resume watching the TV, I stride to a closet where I store a shotgun purchased for home protection.

Pointing the gun down, shaking, I open the door. "What do you want?"

Noticing the gun, they step back. A man with long hair, beady eyes and a pockmarked face says he's looking for a person who sells Ecstasy for me.

"He doesn't live here," I say, hoping they'll leave. "This is my house."

"He owes us money," he says in an insistent tone. "We know he comes here."

Raising my voice, I say, "I don't know how you know he comes here, but he owes me money, too. Two-thousand dollars I gave him for a party, which he hasn't been able to pay back."

"He took money off us to take to San Fran for LSD, and we haven't heard from him since."

"I don't know anything about that. Look, I can't help you. I've got visitors here right now. Please don't come back." I slam the door in their faces and watch them slink away. As this is low on the scale of bad things that can happen to a drug dealer, relief sets in. But as I turn around with the shotgun, I notice my parents gazing at me, their wide eyes glistening with shock. My dad looks as if he's about to fall off the sofa. I freeze for a few seconds. My biggest fear is of them finding out that I'm involved in criminal activity.

"Oh my God!" Mum says.

"What the hell's going on, Shaun?" Dad asks.

Searching for the right words, my mind speeds up. "Just some kids looking for a friend of mine. I didn't know who they were, and you can't take any chances in America. They could have been robbers with guns – that's why I took the shotgun. I really didn't need it. It's all resolved and they left without a problem."

For the rest of the night, my parents remain alarmed. In the following days, they don't mention the incident, so I assume they believe my explanation. Guilt-ridden, I arrange for them to stay at a Jacuzzi suite in a Sedona hotel owned by one of my stockbrokerage clients.

Months later, to avoid any more unexpected knocks on the door, I move into a condominium near the top of a high-security building fitted with laser trip wires and a guard station. I quit my job as a stockbroker to concentrate on dealing Ecstasy. I don't show up for work one day, leaving my colleagues wondering whether I'm dead or alive. Not knowing how to explain the transition to my parents, and feeling awful about the necessity of lying to camouflage my illegal activity, I postpone contacting them. Unfortunately, an ex-colleague calls them. My mum picks up the phone. He asks if she knows where I am. When she says no, he fabricates a story that my car was found burnt out on the Mexican border, insinuating that I may have died. With no way of getting hold of me at my new location, my parents panic and fret over the worst. They contact my aunt in Phoenix, who, days later, manages to get a message to me.

Before calling them, I take a few deep breaths. My mum answers, thankful to hear my voice, but angry about the phone call and my lack of communication. I apologize.

"Can you imagine what it was like for me hearing on the phone that you may have died in a burnt out car? It was one of the worst moments of my life! I had an image in my head of your charred body being discovered, unrecognizable. The guy was so insistent and heartless. What was he doing lying like that to someone's mother? What was he up to?"

"Sounds like he was using shock tactics to try and find out if you knew where I was."

"It was an evil thing to do. Where were you?" she says, raising her voice. "Why didn't you get in touch?"

"He had no right to upset you like that. I'm sorry. I had to go into hiding," I say, immediately regretting my response.

29

"This just gets worse! Hiding! From who?"

"My old firm. I just didn't show up to work. The thought of going in there and officially quitting made me feel ill. I got so sick of having to be in the office for 6am and working such long hours that I've decided to live off my investment portfolio and try throwing raves."

"Raves! What about drugs? I've heard of Ecstasy being taken at raves. You're not involved in any of that are you?" Mum asks in a concerned tone.

"No. We've got security everywhere checking for drugs and bouncers on the doors, so that no drug dealers or underage can get in."

"I'd hate to think of the trouble you'd get into if people sneak drugs in."

"They won't. Don't worry. We've got it covered."

"It's a shame about the stockbroking. You worked so hard to achieve your ambition."

"Most of my wealth is in my stock-market portfolio. Raves are just a sideline."

"Good luck with it all, then," she says as if she believes me.

Six years later, I'm arrested and all of my assets are confiscated. I have no one to turn to other than my family. Deep guilt about the way I've treated them makes me hesitate before stooping to pick up a phone bolted to a jailhouse wall, its cord intentionally short to prevent suicide or murder by strangulation. I dread what's about to happen. My biggest fear is going to be realized: my family are going to know about my criminal activity. To prevent inmates from noticing how upset I am, I pretend to wipe sweat from my face while using my fingers to flick off tears. I desperately don't want to break my parents and sister's hearts, but feel I have no choice but to dial. As their phone rings, my stomach clenches and churns. Fighting the urge to throw up, I greet my sister in a weak uncertain voice.

"Shaun's on the phone!" Karen yells. "What have you done? Mum and Dad are in a proper state. They're worried sick."

"Look, it's not as bad as it sounds," I say, trying to play it down.

"God, I hope not. For Mum and Dad's sake. They don't deserve this, Shaun."

"You'd better let me speak to them," I said, bracing myself.

"Anyway, I hope you're okay in there. It must be a nightmare. Here's Dad. Bye! Love you." Her caring voice reinforces my guilt.

She's right. My parents don't deserve any of this. "Love you, too."

"Are you okay?" Dad asks.

The strain in his voice devastates me. I imagine Mum taking it even worse. I'm appalled at myself. I draw on all of my strength to speak in a normal tone. "I'm in trouble, but I'm fine," I say, concealing my fear and the threat posed by the environment. I've just seen a suspected child molester get beaten to death by the Aryan Brotherhood. He was extracted from our pod on a stretcher with not just blood leaking from his head, but yellow fluid and brain matter.

"Well, we'll do whatever it takes to help you."

Their pledge of support is a relief. Some of my neighbours in jail have been disowned by their families due to drug activity. "They've given me a list of charges, but I haven't a clue what they mean. My bond's $750,000 and I know none of us has that kind of money."

"I know about the bond. I rang the jail."

"What did you find out?"

"It sounds pretty serious. I was on that daft automated line for about forty-five minutes, going around in a loop – press 1, press 2, press 3 – putting your booking number in at different stages, and all of a sudden a voice popped up. I explained the situation to her. As soon as I said, 'I'm calling from England about my son who has been arrested,' she immediately wanted to help me. The English accent has its advantages."

"It does. It's helping me in here. What did she say?"

"I said, 'I can't understand what's happened. I can't believe what's going on or why he's been arrested.' She said, 'Give me his booking number, and I'll find out what I can for you.' She gave me the charges – which I didn't really understand – and then she said, 'The bond is $750,000. This looks pretty serious.'"

That they know the extent of my trouble fills me with panic. "Oh, dear. I'm so sorry. Mum must be worried sick."

"She's bearing up."

"I'd better speak to her then."

"Okay, here she is."

"Shaun, are you safe in there?"

Hearing my mum crying hurts. I detest myself for causing her to suffer. "Yes, I'm alright, Mum."

"What's all this about?"

The more she speaks, the more nauseous I feel.

"I can't really say much on these phones, Mum. I was raided, but no drugs were found. My bond's so big, it doesn't look like I'll be going anywhere anytime soon," I say, struggling to sound composed.

"I can't believe this has happened."

"I know. I'm so sorry," I say, tears streaming down my face.

Her voice calms a bit as she says firmly, "We'll do what we can to help you."

A female computerised voice interrupts the call: "You have 30 seconds remaining."

"It's going to hang up, Mum."

"We love you very, very much. We'll do what we can."

"Love you too. So sorry about all –"

The line goes dead. Disgusted with myself, devastated, I walk away from the phone in a daze.

My parents cashed in their retirement accounts and re-mortgaged their house to come up with almost $100,000 for a lawyer. Facing a 200-year maximum sentence, I entered a court battle that took 26 months. Eventually, I signed a plea bargain for 9½ years. Without a private lawyer, I'd probably still be incarcerated or I may have never gotten out. My party friends owed me hundreds of thousands, but I barely saw a penny of it back. Some of them were glad that I was arrested so they'd never have to repay me.

The money I owe my parents, I'm slowly paying back. What's more difficult to deal with is the psychological damage to my family. When I stay with them, I can still see the hurt and pain on their faces that I caused through the stress of my incarceration and criminal behaviour. People sometimes ask, "Shaun, you've lived a wild and crazy life. Is there anything about it you would have changed?" Automatically, I reply, "Yes, as well as regretting putting people on the road of drug use, I'd like to take the stress and pain away from my family, but I can't. It makes me sick to my stomach, and it's something I've got to live with for the rest of my life."

The recent publication of my memoir, *Party Time*, caused a much bigger reaction in my family than I had anticipated. Reading about the irresponsible choices I made that led to my arrest and that devastated all of our lives resurfaced their hurt. My dad is still suffering. He has a mellow disposition and rarely talks to me about his feelings. When I asked him to express himself for this book, he replied: "Reading *Party Time* made me angry again, because it reminded me of all the stupid things you did, which in turn led to your sentencing. I'm still angry because of what you did to your mum and sister. I doubt if either of them will ever get over it. You turned a normal family into one that is associated with serious criminality. And we had to do things we never should have had to. This is something we all have to live with in spite of all the jokes and black humour surrounding it all. Forgiveness comes easy to a parent; forgetting is far more difficult."

My mother didn't react as severely to *Party Time* as my father because she edited it and was familiar with my wrongdoings. After she finished editing, I added a few new scenes. Reading those shocked her. I asked her, "Since my arrest, what have you read that's affected you the most?" She replied that the most devastating thing she ever read about me was an article in the *Phoenix New Times*, published a few months after my arrest. On the cover was a portrait of me as the vampire Nosferatu, extending my arms around some of my co-conspirators. The article was ten pages long. It contained everything I'd ever done and ten times more. They portrayed me to be a cross between Tony Soprano and a vampire. Although I told my parents that the story was exaggerated, my mother said reading it was a massive shock. Appalled, grief-stricken and terrified of the story making the UK press, she went into shops glancing furtively at newspaper headlines. She was afraid of people finding out and smashing the windows of her house and daubing graffiti on the walls along the lines of DRUG DEALERS. She never told anyone, not even the people at the college she worked at, until one day she broke down. Spotting a group of foreign students sitting outside of the staff room, she got it into her head that they'd read the article. Confronting them, she shouted, "You know all about it! You've read the *New Times*!" She ran around the room screaming. My father came to collect her. She'd had a nervous breakdown and was put on medication. Counselling, yoga and meditation has helped her deal with the sadness and the anger she felt towards me.

Guilt over what I've put my family through weighs heavily on my heart, but it also motivates me to do well in life. I can't change the past, but I can certainly stay on a positive track.

Since my release, my family have shown strong support for all of my endeavours. It was my mum's idea to start doing book signings at Waterstones, which put me on the map as an author. Despite their reluctance to relive my story, my parents both said "yes" right away when asked if they would be willing to be filmed for my *Locked-Up/Banged-Up Abroad* episode. Just today, a journalist from Yahoo! is at my parents' house interviewing them about the family side of my story. Repeatedly, they have sacrificed their time and well-being to help keep my life on track, including their contributions to this book. So far my family has read the prologue and the first three chapters and offered feedback. They've been paying particular attention to this chapter as it has engaged their emotions the most. My mum is feeling drained from it. She just emailed, "I need a break from all this now. I'm fed up with it. It's getting me down. So don't send anything else to me for at least a week."

I mentioned earlier about doing well in the future. This book is a statement of that. It reinforces what I'm doing and what I'm about in a positive framework. It puts my negative behaviour in the context of my transformation. I'm hoping that the finished product will help my family view me in a more positive way.

When a catastrophe befalls a family, it can bring you closer together or pull you apart. You blame yourself or you blame each other, but in the end you have to accept what has happened and give each other support.

Here's a quote from a letter I wrote home during my second year in the jail:

One of the themes of the philosophy books is how short our time on earth is. How when we die, we don't get to take our material possessions with us. To love and be loved by our family and friends during our brief lifetimes seems to be the point of the ancient philosophers.

Lesson 4:
Identify and Overcome Addictions

"Rule your desires lest your desires rule you."
– Publilius Syrus

It's 1997 and I'm high on a club-drug cocktail at a rave in a massive downtown Phoenix warehouse. A stranger offers me a mystery pill he calls a Funeral Wreath. Looking to push myself further into oblivion, I don't hesitate to take it.

Forty or so minutes later, I collapse onto the dusty cement floor. With so much activity around me, no one notices the trouble I'm in. My throat starts constricting. *If I don't drink water, I'm going to die* is all I can think. I spot a plastic water bottle containing a few gulps about ten feet away and start crawling towards it. A third of the way, I feel the strength drain from my body. *I'm running out of time.* Breathing awkwardly, panicking, I only manage to move a few inches. Ravers stride around me as if I'm a log. Some trip over me. Hoping to regain my strength, I take a rest, sucking in as much air as possible through my constricted throat. My friends are dancing in other rooms. I pray one finds me. Starting to hallucinate, I flinch at the avalanche of sneakers at the height of my head, cartoonlike, dangerously close.

My dry throat feels as if it's choking the life from me. *Surely, I'm not going to die surrounded by so many. If only someone would help me and give me a drink.* Having never felt so thirsty in my life, I muster all of my willpower to keep budging towards the water. My fingers scratch and scrape the concrete. A few inches at a time, I force my reluctant body forward. Managing to advance a couple of feet takes an eternity and saps the last of my strength. Watching a raver kick the bottle further away kills my hope. My brain's instructions to move are ignored by my body. Giving up on the bottle, I hand myself over to fate. Due to the discomfort of breathing against the floor, I roll into the position of a beetle trapped on its back. My throat closes so tight it feels like a chord is tightening around it. Convinced I have limited time to stay alive, I strain to raise my head, but it feels ten times heavier than normal. With tremendous effort, I lift it a few inches. I look around for my friends as my hallucinations intensify: people blend into each other, merging unrecognizably as their bodies liquefy. My neck gives out. *Thump!* My head hits the cement. Every time I manage to raise my head, it hovers a few inches and slams back down painfully. My skull can only take so much. I stop trying. Within minutes, I can't move, not even my fingers. Terrified, I concentrate on breathing to stay alive. Praying someone finds me right now, I watch my eyelids close. The world blackens.

I regain consciousness in a friend's arms, outside. He has two heads. The sky is a blend of night and day. Flying cars are joined to clouds by drainpipes. I try to speak, but no words emerge. I don't know if I'm dead or alive.

The following Monday, still subject to hallucinations, I wake up to a bedroom ceiling covered in squiggling bacteria. I curse the mystery pill and swear never to take drugs again. By Friday, I'm craving drugs. All I can think about is getting high.

Eight years later, having requested psychotherapy, I'm at the Medical Unit in prison, wondering whether the doctor will be a pill pusher or someone I can make progress with in a holistic fashion. A guard escorts me into a small room with no windows, a beat-up desk and a man dressed in a blue shirt and black trousers. He's tall with a penetrating stare; his brown hair is tinged grey at the front and above the ears, his beard white. Speaking slowly, he introduces himself as Dr. Owen, a cognitive behaviourist and neuropsychologist.

I tell him about my background, that I was raised by great parents, loving and kind, who grew up in the hippie culture of the sixties. I was the centre of their attention until my sister came along, and perhaps that's why I teased her a lot. Although further education was frowned upon in our industrial hometown, our parents encouraged it. I describe my love of yoga and how I read philosophy and psychology in the hope of helping my personal development. I say that I mostly took club drugs – Ecstasy, ketamine and speed – and that my drug intake reached dangerous levels during relationship breakdowns. I speculate that getting arrested probably saved my life. Although I'd quit dealing and was trying to wean myself off drugs, something probably would have happened to trigger yet another self-destructive binge.

He reassures me that his talk-therapy approach attempts to address the root causes of psychological disturbances, whereas pills often only address the symptoms. He's studied

Eastern philosophy and yoga. He says that I obtained a definition of who I was through partying. The drugs I took caused a cascade of neurotransmitters that made my anxiety go away, but my brain was operating at a dangerous level due to the huge amounts of chemicals in my system. He advises me to study yoga books and in particular to consider my connection to the universal. He wants me to start a journal of positive and negative thoughts to raise my awareness of my thinking.

I leave the session on a high, feeling that I have more chemistry with Dr. Owen than any other staff I've come across in prison. In my cell, I open a yoga book. It says that I'm a small part of something larger than me: the universe. Staring at my living quarters – two bunks and a combination sink/toilet – I feel utterly disconnected from the universe. No matter how many times I tell myself that I'm part of it, nothing happens. If anything, I feel abandoned by it. On Ecstasy, I felt connected to people and nature. Breathing felt divine. I wonder why I'm not happy in my natural state.

I gaze out of the tiny window at the back of the cell at a giant chain-link fence topped with razor wire. Armed guards on patrol drive by in a truck, shining a light into the no-man's-land area of the dust bowl between the fence and my building where potential escapees are subject to being shot. The sight reminds me how enclosed I am and adds to my frustration. I wonder if yoga will teach me to feel normal.

Confused, I put my faith in Dr. Owen, trusting that he'll help decipher my nature, so I can avoid my previous mistakes.

A month later, I arrive to see Dr. Owen, eager to make progress, but unsure where psychotherapy is heading.

"Before we begin, is there anything you'd like to discuss?" he asks.

"Yes, there is. I'd like to get your advice about drugs. Obviously, I don't need to be running around raves doing designer drugs. But where do I draw the line? It seems everyone in the world is on drugs if you include alcohol, tobacco and prescription pills. Can I drink a glass of wine with my parents over dinner? Can I take Xanax before flying for anxiety?"

"There are two things you need to think about. Firstly, you need awareness and mindfulness to understand the situations and circumstances that are drawing you to drugs. Secondly, you need an awareness of how drugs work. On the wall behind me is a diagram of the limbic system, a system of nerves and networks that when stimulated makes you feel good and tells you, *Let's get higher and higher*. Doing more drugs gives you immediate gratification. Instead of seeking such chemically induced extremes, you must learn how to activate such feelings at lower natural levels. Ecstasy, ketamine, or whatever doesn't come in nature. They are refined substances that cause huge cascades of neurotransmitters. You need to think about what gives you a little euphoria without doing drugs."

"Are you saying any kind of drug is out of the question? What if I want to take a one-time trip to do peyote with North Mexican Indians or Amanita mushrooms with Siberians? I read about professional people who occasionally take these trips as consciousness-raising experiments," I countered.

"Why would Mexican Indians or indigenous Siberians want you, some Westerner, sharing their sacred rituals?"

"Are you saying they'd only be doing it for commercial reasons?"

"Which leads to problems. You're assuming you can buy a cheap thrill through a mystical experience. A mystical experience is supposed to give you a profound understanding of the universe."

"Timothy Leary claimed to get that through LSD."

"Maybe he did, but my answer for you is a resounding no! There are no short cuts for you. Ahead is a journey down a long hard road that's going to get you where you need to be. If you do drugs once, you'll want to test yourself again and again. You'll think, *I can do this and this.* When in actuality your willpower is messed up by drugs. Your neurotransmitters are screwed up by huge chemical loads in the brain. You'll have to become like a teetotaller who learns to appreciate tea, or a highly sexual person who learns to have sex with one partner, allowing your partner to look into yourself. Yoga will help. You need to find things that make sense to you and explore those to achieve unity."

"Writing and creativity make sense." Reading and writing occupy most of my time in prison. I feel passionate about them.

"There are many authors who have done drugs and done well. But they did drugs to address inner turmoil, and when they looked back after doing drugs they saw they had natural writing skills regardless of the drugs."

"I've had inner turmoil."

"That's something you need to figure out."

I breathe deeply. "At times of extreme stress, I heard wolves howling for me to come out and party," I say, hoping I don't sound crazy.

He nods for me to continue.

"Over time, I figured they represent my raver friends all combined into a strong force. Certain rave music also triggers the wolves. If I stayed in on a weekend, they howled so loud for me to come out that I couldn't sit still or rest and, more often than not, I'd follow their call and find a party. When I got to a party and was with my raver friends, getting high, the wolves shut up and left me alone."

"And what of the wolves now?"

"After my arrest, I didn't have time to think about them,

but today with you, some of the questions I asked were derived from their influence, which must mean there's still a part of me that wants to party. I feel like I've become a new person because of everything that's happened since my arrest, but another part of me is struggling to accept that, and I'm afraid of that part." I've never expressed my feelings so deeply with anyone. Tensed-up, I gaze, hoping his response will make a difference in my life.

"You need to go back, way back, and ask yourself what you were telling yourself from the ages of 12 to 25. How old were you when you first started to hear the wolves?"

I remember driving around when I'd first arrived in Phoenix in 1991. Having not yet made many friends, I felt lonely and homesick. Playing tapes of rave music I recorded in the UK, I longed to party, but I didn't know where to go. That's when I started to hear the wolves. "Early twenties," I say, shifting awkwardly in my seat, uncomfortable for having revealed the wolves to someone for the first time.

"That's when your personality solidified and you chose certain paths in life. There was something about you that you were not happy with and perhaps you filled that gap with the wolves."

"I'm not sure. I've always been happy-go-lucky. In school a lot of boys grew bigger and taller than me, and I felt inadequate until I caught up. I got mauled by some of the rugby players, but nothing major. As I grew, I preferred the company of girlfriends. I was always a wheeler-dealer from a young age, and that drive got stronger, much stronger into my early twenties."

"Why do you feel you were driven to acquire material things?"

"I guess I had something to prove. I set out to conquer Wall Street with a 100% faith in my ability. I equated success and material stuff with my stock market goal."

"So you were mesmerized by external things, and you didn't give much attention to your inner core. There's a part of you that wanted attention, and material things would generate that. You need to realize the essence of a person has nothing to do with being attracted to money and things. Look at the Dalai Lama. He looks like a regular old fella. But he's very charismatic. You need to find your internal self, and ask yourself, *What person do I want to be?* Drugs aren't going to do that for you. Not peyote or mescaline or LSD. Hallucinogens may fit into certain cultures, but in our culture they don't make sense."

Resistance towards his response rises up within me, tightening my body. "Does all the alcohol and nicotine consumption make sense?"

"Wasn't that a scene you were part of?"

"No! We were counterculture. We dressed outrageously. Our music sounded like signals from outer space. We were rebellious. We sneered at mainstream, including mainstream drugs. We were out to shock."

"Is this the wolves talking?"

He's right. Wishing I could retract what I said and feeling foolish, I laugh.

"You wanted attention," he says.

"I got attention."

"But it didn't work out. Everything you did was a step on the path that brought you here."

"That's true."

"With increased mindfulness, you can learn from the previous negative things you did and determine what things are going to be beneficial to you. You're able to start afresh."

"I agree," I say, feeling more hopeful and relaxed.

"Do you realize that anxiety has driven you all your life? You need to be able to learn to listen to your anxiety. To know when things make sense and when they stop making sense. If anxiety causes you irrational thoughts, remember to breathe. Long deep breaths. Make Darth Vader noises if you have to."

Having told him about the wolves, I return to my cell feeling unburdened. I realize he's right about my lifelong anxiety. When it rises, I make bad choices. I wonder what's at the root of it and whether it's genetic as my mum suffers from anxiety and depression. I'm hopeful that after prison I'll view the world as a safer place and my anxiety will subside.

In the next session, Dr. Owen examines my homework:

What I was thinking when I was high on drugs at raves, and how I presently think about these actions.

On drugs at a rave I'm having the time of my life. Everyone is having fun. My friends are behaving as bizarrely as can be. There are thousands dancing to electronic beats, European style. I'm getting hugged and thanked for organizing the party and supplying Ecstasy. I'm excited about the after-party I'm throwing and the extremes of human behaviour and drug taking that will happen. My wife is kissing a girlfriend, turning me on. I'm high on GHB, Special K, and Xanax. I'm starting to feel the hit of Ecstasy. I'm rushing. My skin feels warm and fuzzy. I can't stop smiling. Life is divine. The music and my heartbeat are moving in sync. Gooseflesh is rippling across my skin. Just breathing, tasting air, I feel so alive. I never want it to end.

How I think now: At the rate I partied, I'm lucky to be alive. That lifestyle starts out as fun, but leads to trouble and incarceration. I was emotionally immature. I've developed other interests I enjoy such as writing. I hope to use my knowledge in positive ways and to help prisoners. No more drugs and wild partying. Incarceration was meant to *happen to force me to grow up, educate me, and to show me the error of my ways. To accomplish positive things, I can't screw up my decision-making processes; otherwise I won't succeed in life or as a writer.*

"It seems," Dr. Owen says, "you've compared and contrasted your present thoughts with your past actions. You've realized if you go back to partying, it's not going to do you any good. You'll also have to look more closely at the decisions that led you to the substance-abuse lifestyle."

"Earlier in my life when I felt shy, drugs enabled me to socialize. I figured I'd do them for fun, mostly on the weekends, and quit whenever I wanted."

"Do you consider yourself a drug addict?"

"No," I say, offended. "I'm not a heroin addict who wakes up and sticks a needle in his arm, who has to get high every day or else feels ill. I was a functional recreational drug user. I'd party all weekend and work on the weekdays."

Dr. Owen shakes his head. "Addiction is when doing drugs interferes with your ability to function. When doing drugs interferes with your life. Take a look around you. Where are you right now?"

"Prison."

"What brought you here?"

"Choosing to do drugs." For the first time my denial is finally lifted. I blush, yet feel empowered because now that I've identified my addiction, I'm more likely to recover from it.

"If you weren't addicted to drugs, you wouldn't be here. You have a narrow view. Acknowledging your addiction exists is difficult for you. You must look at it in terms of how you would introduce yourself at an AA meeting: 'I'm Shaun. I'm a drug addict. I've been clean and sober for so many years.'"

Although I'm pleased with the progress with Dr. Owen, back in my cell I resist being labelled an addict. Books I've read compare addiction to a lifelong disease with the addict at constant risk of relapse. The more I ponder the word addict, the more unpalatable it becomes. But I can't deny it either. Its reality surrounds me. The majority of my neighbours are injecting drugs. They're stuck in a cycle of addiction that's too hard to break. Even under the threat of losing their health and lives to hepatitis C – which two-thirds of them contracted in prison – they're ruled by their addictions. The ones I see get released with positive goals usually relapse and return. *If the end of the road for addicts is prison and death, it's a road I'm not going any further down.* Having dealt drugs, I'm ashamed for sending people down that road. As I can't reverse my past, I pledge to use my experience to help others from making my mistakes.

Months later, I ask Dr. Owen, "What's the single most important piece of advice you can give me?"

"You need to be willing to accept who you are. Don't always want to be better, or new and improved. You contain a lot of good inside you. You're doing a good job of sorting yourself out. You're putting tremendous effort into it. Make haste slowly. Don't let your abundant energy distract you. Don't destroy yourself. Don't rush down the path. You'll do exceptionally well if you don't get confused, and if you realize what's going on around you, and how it could affect you. Be cognizant of the pluses and minuses – the consequences of your actions. Learn about yourself from yoga. Over the next year, focus on several poses, the alignment, the breathing, the micro-adjustments, the fluency of the poses themselves. A foundation will develop, not just muscle on bone, but a strong foundation from which you'll know yourself better and be able to expand in all directions. From your physical practice, you'll develop a mental foundation. Developing into quite a nice person is the goal."

"A final thing: what about the wolves?"

"You have to decide where to channel that energy. If you channel it into your previous negative addictions, you'll end up back in here. If you channel it into the positive ones you've cultivated such as yoga and writing, you'll thrive."

Afterwards in my cell, I realize that the wolves – whom I viewed as my friends – are a reflection of my addictions. Thanks to Dr. Owen, the wolves have lost their strength over me.

In 2008, recently released from prison, I substitute an illegal addiction with a legal one by turning to alcohol. Having not touched booze for six years, my system isn't used to it. I drink a few pints of Guinness, pass out and wake up on a pub bench, staring at the ceiling. For almost a year, I go out and get drunk with my friends. I justify my behaviour by telling myself, *At least I'm off the drugs.* Long forgotten is the most wizened cellmate I ever had in the county jail. When I first met him I assumed he was a heroin, meth or crack addict around 70-years old until he revealed he was a 40-something alcoholic who drank hard liquor every day as soon as he woke up.

Drinking alcohol is so sewn into the fabric of what's socially acceptable – even though it's the biggest killer of men in the UK under 50 and alcohol is the most common drug involved in violent crime and rape – it seems abnormal not to drink. It's difficult for me to see the harm I'm doing to myself. But as I progress with yoga and meditation as prescribed by Dr. Owen, I realize I'm using alcohol to fill a void.

Part of the void is the stress of readjusting to society. Psychiatrist and Holocaust survivor Viktor Frankl compared the turmoil caused by getting released from prison to a diver coming up with the bends. During the year following my release, there are times when I worry that everything I've been through has made me seriously mentally ill. There are occasions when my ability to concentrate freezes and all I can do is to curl up on my bed in the foetal position, wondering if I'll ever return to normal.

As I slowly adapt, my tension diminishes. The cost of drinking – headachy hangovers and days of writing lost as I lie on my bed in a daze – starts to outweigh the benefits, much to the horror of some of my friends, who insist I booze with them. I know they just want me to enjoy myself, but I'm starting to prefer my natural state.

The person who inspires me to completely quit drinking is Tony, one of my instructors in BodyCombat, an energetic aerobics class in which I jump, kick and punch to thumping dance music in room with 60 women. At social functions, when everyone has at least one glass of wine in their hands, Tony is drinking juice or water. When I ask him why he doesn't drink, he says that he wants to be as healthy as possible. I'm astounded that he's the life and soul of the party and stays up until the small hours without alcohol or stimulants. Impressed by his natural energy, I tell myself, *It can be done!* I start to wean myself off booze. Now when I join people at a bar, I say in a jocular tone, "Order me a pint of water please." They stare at me with the same wide eyes I once looked at Tony. Having not touched alcohol in two years, I feel much healthier. With no hangover on Sundays, I can actually enjoy the day, instead of being reduced to mush on my bed like an amoeba with a headache.

Ending my schools talks, I describe how Dr. Owen taught me to channel my energy into positive things. I tell the students that from time to time, I still hear the wolves howling for me to come out and party, especially when I hear old-school rave music or a good DJ on the radio. A jolt of excitement runs up my spine and gooseflesh ripples across my skin. At such times, Dr. Owen's advice takes affect like a circuit breaker. It interrupts my urge to yield to the wolves. I choose to take that energy to the fitness centre, where I do a range of classes.

I like to use an extreme example on the students: "Based on what I told you about Dr. Owen, how could you possibly turn your life around if you're the kind of person who likes to walk up to strangers, punch them in the face and get in fights? Well, if you take that energy and channel it into boxing or martial arts, you could get awarded prizes for it instead of ending up with a criminal record that might damage your career prospects. Overcoming any addiction is a case of channelling your energy elsewhere, whether it is drugs, alcohol, gambling or violence."

Exercise releases healthy brain chemicals. Through experience, I've learned how to score the good stuff from my internal pharmacy. During BodyCombat, I thoroughly enjoy the dance music. Afterwards, I feel like I've been raving. With endorphins elevating my mood, I'm high without the Ecstasy. And I sleep much better.

No matter how loud the wolves howl, I start my weekends with three hours of karate on Friday night. After 10pm, I leave the dojo dressed in a karate suit and with a bo staff that's taller than me hitched to my back. Walking from my car to my house, I pass a pub. By this time, the beer garden is packed with noisy revellers eager to make a sport out of heckling me with jokes revolving around "Grasshopper," and the "Karate Kid." With a big smile, I greet them with "Osu!" and bow my head. Osu is an expression used in Japanese martial arts that means "I understand" or "I follow." It's used to show respect to the sensei as you bow and enter the dojo. Judging from their laughter, the revellers seem to appreciate this. It would be easy to join them and get drunk on a Friday night, but instead, I return home with a sense of achievement and no impending hangover.

Thanks to Dr. Owen forcing me to take an inventory of all of my activity, I'm hooked on posit My Coffee Man ive addictions.

Lesson 5:
Learn From Setbacks

"We cannot learn without pain."
– Aristotle

It's a Friday night in July 2013 and I'm heading to karate in a thick white uniform and a brown belt tied tight around my waist. With the UK hosting a rare heat wave, I'm hoping that we don't do anything too strenuous, so that I have plenty of energy to get through three hours of training.

In the dojo, we line-up in formation facing our sensei. He instructs us through stretching exercises and we move onto various punches and kicks. About thirty minutes in, he tells me and another brown belt to join him at the front, and the rest to form a line. I'm instructed to fight everyone in the line, one-on-one, without a rest in-between the fights. As this is my first ever line-up and I feel fear and anxiety over sparring, I tense up. My pulse jumps. My jaw clenches. Sweat trickles down my back. Sparring in recent years, I've broken three fingers and injured my ribs multiple times. Each injury rendered me unable to exercise for up to two months. I wonder whether my reluctance is due to the injuries and my frustration at not being able to exercise during the down time. As I'm training for a black belt, I realize that I must buckle down and get on with the fights.

"The rules are," my sensei says, "you can't attack. You can only block, get the hell out of the way or absorb the blows."

The first fight is with the lowest grade belt in the dojo. I can see in his eyes that he's wary. Unable to attack, I hold my fists far out towards him, hoping he'll run into them if he charges at me too aggressively.

Egged on by comments like, "He can't fight back! Beat the shit out of him!" he launches forward.

Trying to dodge him, I jump and skip around, expending too much energy. When we clash, my adrenaline spikes. I block him hard, trying to use the force of my forearms to push him away. He lands a few good punches, but nothing in the injury zone.

The sensei calls time. I'm panting.

The second fight is with the next grade up. I try the same strategy. Lots of pushing with my blocking arms, which are starting to feel sore from all of the bone-on-bone contact, and skipping away. With my energy subsiding, I'm breathing awkwardly. I open myself up to more blows. Getting hit and being unable to hit back is frustrating. By the end of the fight, I'm more short of breath.

The third fight is with a woman with a gentle nature. I opt to absorb her blows rather than skip around in the hope of regaining my breath. But when the fight ends, I'm still panting like a dog.

The fourth fight is with a recent black belt, shorter than me and well-built. He charges at me, throwing relentless blows. Normally, I'd lash out with my long arms and legs in the hope of keeping him at bay, but I can't attack. I circle away, but he trails the arc of my footsteps, staying on top of me, unleashing blow after blow. My frustration at being unable to attack boils into anger. My energy is spent. Unable to shift quickly in any direction, I receive the most blows I've ever took in karate. I feel like a punching bag. My brain snaps. I try and push him over with a block, accompanied by a sneaky knee to the stomach. He only relents for a few seconds.

"No kicking!" our sensei yells.

I can only stand, exhausted, breathless, while he demolishes my mid-section.

The fifth fight is with another recent black belt. Two months ago, he did a thirty-minute line-up against black belts for his grading. During the third fight, his skull was fractured below the eye by a kick to the head, and he fought on with double vision that only cleared up a few weeks ago. After enduring the two-day grading, he went straight to a hospital.

He comes at me the same as the last, knocking me around the dojo with repeated blows.

Pushed to an extreme, I start hyperventilating.

"I can't breathe properly," I say, leaning on him, half falling over, hoping for mercy.

"We've got to keep going," he says in an encouraging tone.

"I can't. I can't…" I say as the blows continue.

Probably feeling sorry for me, he lightens the blows.

I don't expect the final fight. I think the line-up is over – until the sensei punches me in the chest.

Dazed, I just stumble and reel from the force of his blows, protesting that I can't breathe and I've got no energy. Near the end of the fight, I'm so exhausted that I have neither the breath nor energy to whine. When he announces the end, my mind is absent. I walk to a corner of the dojo, feeling defeated and humiliated. I lie down, a heaving sweaty mass with my hands trembling as if I have Parkinson's disease. I flashback to an incident in 1988…

I'm in my late teens and I've not long passed my driver's test. I'm taking my mum's little red car to a petrol station to fill the tank up. On the forecourt, four drunks in their twenties built like rugby players start kicking my car. Instead of getting in the car and driving off, I yell at them to stop.

They surround me. Immediately, I regret not fleeing. Helplessly trapped, I feel my stomach plunge. *How bad is this going to get?* They toy with me like cats on an injured bird. One lunges. I leap out of his way, but almost back into another. Trying to keep an eye on all of them, I swivel from side to side with heightened awareness and my pulse roaring in my ears. Whichever direction I shift towards, they shadow me, so that I'm constantly surrounded. The force of a shoe against the back of my knee takes my leg out. They fall upon me, flattening me against the hard concrete. I scramble to get up, but their painful blows keep me down. My initial instinct is to resist and try to flee. But every direction I flip and flop towards exposes my stomach to kicks. Switching into damage-limitation mode, I stop resisting. My front can't take any more blows, so I curl my body forward. They focus on my head, kicking it like a football. Each time a shoe makes contact with my skull I feel an explosion of pain as if I'm shot in the head. There's blood on my hands. I pray that their aggression has peaked. One swings an iron bar that I don't see until it hits my face, knocking pieces of my teeth out, sending a scalding pain through my jaw, skull and down my spine. I see white flashes and stars. It dawns that they're not beating me up. *I'm getting murdered.* Going into shock, I try to shield my face from the iron bar. It strikes my arm, which burns with hot pain. I clench my eyes the tightest they've ever been. I hug my head and bury my face in the joints of my arms. Blow after blow rains down, each one sending a scorching shockwave of pain down from my skull and leaving a ringing noise in my ears as if gunshots are going off in close proximity. My entire body heats up, absorbing the pain until it's no longer felt. I feel as if I'm abandoning my body to escape from the blows. *This is what dying feels like.* I'm appalled at myself for yelling at the drunks. I can't believe my life's ending so unexpectedly at such an early age. I can still feel blows making contact, so I don't remove my arms from my head, but there's no pain. The longer they carry on, the more I feel my life ebbing away. It reaches a point where I just want it to end. Feeling warm and no longer afraid, I surrender to the inevitable and pass out.

On the pavement, I wake up covered in blood. Remembering what happened, I raise my sore weary head to scan the area for my assailants. No sign of them. I spit out teeth parts and strings of blood. I run my thumb over my front teeth and feel jagged pieces. The car windscreen is smashed. I hear the garage attendant yelling. A police car speeds past with a siren blaring. Terrified my assailants might return, I limp to my car and drive home. Shocked by the state of my face, my parents insist on taking me to a hospital.

Until recently, I kept the beating by the drunks a secret. After my teeth were fixed, I blocked it out. On the floor in the karate dojo, I get a notion that the beating is at the root of my resistance to sparring. I also suspect that it's one of the causes of the anxiety that Dr. Owen pointed out has ruled my life. Getting punched in such an intense way returned me to that day as if I were getting almost murdered again. The line-up provoked a breakthrough in understanding that I've been seeking all of my life.

The day after the karate line-up, I wake up hyper aware of my body. All day, I contemplate the psychological consequences. Hoping to make progress, I arrange to meet my meditation teacher to discuss it further.

For almost a year, I've been attending Andrew's meditation class every Sunday. He doesn't charge as he believes in helping others. I never thought I'd meet someone like Dr. Owen, but Andrew is in the same league of people with wisdom gleaned from vast experience. Andrew is tall with thick dark brows and an intelligent face below slightly greying hair swept back. Thanks to a Lebanese father, he's blessed with skin that looks tanned all year round. That he's meditated for over 30 years is apparent in the tranquillity in his brown eyes. They sparkle when he gets animated. When he's not power-dressed for his job as a criminal defence lawyer, complete with a silk scarf and embroidered handkerchief, he's usually in a pink T-shirt and slacks. His voice inflexion is unique, ranging from a baritone to a soft clear whisper. The hypnotic quality of his voice increases the slower he talks until his words feel as if they're melting into my ears and dripping into my subconscious. My personal development has accelerated under him. We often meet for lunch. After seeing him, I always leave on a high, with things that have been weighing on my mind for weeks falling into place.

At an Indian restaurant, I tell Andrew what happened in karate and how I was once nearly beaten to death, not in prison or by the Mafia, but a few miles from my home at a petrol station by drunks.

"Life presents us with challenges," he says. "Life normally identifies our weak areas, emotional, physical and spiritual, and gives us a situation and the opportunity to grow in those areas. But rather than take the opportunity, most of us hide the experience away in our subconscious and supress it. The whole point is to face it and experience growth in that area."

"Which I didn't do when I was almost beaten to death because I was too young to understand any of this stuff."

"You repressed it, and it's been lying dormant like a dark area on your subconscious. The longer you ran away from it, the weaker you became in that area. It's like an insidious growth that continues to expand while you keep running. In karate, you were forced into a situation where this area you've been repressing was brought to the surface and you had to observe it because it was so bloody painful. Your subconscious may have influenced you to begin karate to deal with this issue from your past. The subconscious does influence and to some degree manipulate us for good and ill, depending on which aspect is at play."

"That attack was so long ago, twenty-five years. I'd forgotten it was there."

"At karate you were pushed to your limit and your fear was brought to the surface. It was your fear that exhausted you and your resistance to the content at the subconscious level. You were running away from that issue."

"I did! I had the urge to run away from the dojo, but I couldn't."

"The purpose of martial arts is to bring you into the present moment, which you couldn't experience because you were dealing with the issue. The great thing is that it was brought to the surface, which burst its bubble. You don't need to run away any longer. You need to drink the experience. You need to ask yourself, *What's the lesson I've learned from this?* It was extremely harsh for someone so young to go through such an awful experience. Now you know to face the demons within you and not turn away. The whole process has taught you courage."

"I don't think I learned anything from it at the time. I put it aside, and never thought about it until karate."

"Were there any incidents to do with fights or confrontation when you were growing up?"

"I'm non-confrontational. In secondary school, I was quickly put in place by the rugby players. I was a skinny nerd to them. I used to hide out in the technical-drawing room reading the *Financial Times* rather than go to break and risk getting beaten up."

"From a spiritual perspective, there's a journey for you to take as a consequence of this incident. Severe pain takes you to a place within yourself that is your true self. You become the observer detached from the physical body."

"It did feel as if I'd left my body."

"The way to resolve this now is to seek the experience back out again, so you can stop carrying the pain of that incident."

"How do I do that?"

"It's been done for you. The fight forced it to the surface, but now you must seek it out yourself. Go down there. Relive it. Breathe in the negative energy of the experience and turn it into a positive. What you breathe in will make you stronger. Ask yourself, *Why did I have this experience and what did it teach me about myself?* It's great that karate exposed this issue as it was eating away at your subconscious."

"On the subject of using negative experiences as transformative and not repressing them, I'm working on a self-help book and the publisher has asked me to write about any feelings that have been brought to the surface in my family. My dad supports me as much as possible, but he never goes to any of my talks because he doesn't want to relive it. He rarely talks about the pain my incarceration put him through. My mum and I talk about it a lot. I can see on his face that it's hurting him inside. How can I help him deal with it?"

"The reason he's hurting is because of love for you. For a parent to see their child go through that degree of suffering hurts the parent more than the child. He's experienced dreadful emotional pain on your behalf. Rather than relive it and purge it, he's supressing it. He doesn't want to deal with it because it's so painful. The only way you can influence him is with the clarity and purity of your love. As you continue to change yourself, your expression of love will expand and extend to him"

"I take full responsibility for all of the awful things I put my family through. All I can do is give them love and show them what I'm doing now."

"The only thing you can do is ensure that the experience you went through enhances your own spiritual journey. You cannot transform other people's opinions. In order to compensate them, you must progress as much as you can. Don't let the opinions of others hold you back. We deal with situations not by lashing out, but by using the negative as a transformative experience, which is what you've done with your incarceration. Your behaviour put you in prison where there was suffering. Rather than run away from it and supress it, or take more drugs and avoid it like many do in prison, you took it head on. You thought, *What is there to learn from this experience? I'm guilty. I'm responsible. I take my punishment. But I'll now use it as a positive experience in my life.* You went beyond the guilt, and thought, *How can this improve me? How can I grow stronger spiritually and as a person? How can I move outside of the ego, the individual small self, and expand myself as a consequence of what's happened?* You used it to grow outside of the parameters of your former self. It's now a positive experience in your life and that's a successful transformative effect. All suffering is exactly the same. If someone causes you to suffer, don't project that negativity back. Ask yourself, *How can*

I take this to make me grow spiritually? If someone hurts you emotionally, don't retaliate. Think, *Why am I being hurt emotionally? What is the experience for me? Why is it hurting me emotionally? What am I attached to? What are my fears in this relationship?* An aspect of love between two people is the desire to help them expand."

"A final question," I say. "I recently went to a neuro-science lecture. The speaker said to forget about all of the Freudian raking up of the past. Forgetting is therapeutic. How do you reconcile that with delving into the subconscious to release repressed emotional pain?"

"As far as I can tell in my present state of knowledge, in order to access your true self you have to go through the subconscious. The first stage is to stop supressing the contents of the subconscious. Whatever arises from the subconscious, there is absolutely no point in reliving the past. But it certainly doesn't involve forgetting it. You allow it to arise. You remain still and you allow the experience to pass. Afterwards, you can talk about the experience in order to process it logically with reason, seeing, for example, if it has an influence over your present life. But there's no need to relive it, only to understand it. Your speaker said, 'Forgetting is therapeutic.' If you're going through a particularly stressful period, it may well be wise for the doctor to give you drugs to allow you to re-centre yourself. So in some sense, forgetting can be therapeutic, but it's also incredibly dangerous because if you completely forget what you're doing, then you're supressing. You have to acknowledge the contents of the subconscious because if you supress them they are going to express themselves somehow. If you keep running away from the contents of your subconscious, these are your fears."

"I think you're right because that's what's happened in my life. People say to me all the time at the schools and stuff, 'Shaun, you come across as this vibrant happy person with good energy. How do you reconcile that with telling us horror stories that happened in the jail? How can you be like this? Don't you relive it every time?' And I say, 'By not holding it in, I'm unburdening myself. That my story is being used for good to inspire people helps my well-being and gives me a larger sense of purpose. If I'd stored what happened inside myself and not worked through it in terms of not just the talks, but meditation and other ways I've worked on it, then I'd be like some ex-prisoners I've seen who refuse to talk about incarceration. They have tension about them that is triggered by anything prison-related.'"

"How this works is this," Andrew says. "You make a mistake in your life. A so-called mistake. Bear in mind that we're talking about relative moral values here. You make an error and you deny that aspect of yourself. There's good and bad in all of us. What we tend to do is only acknowledge that which is good about us, our strengths, while denying the existence of that which is apparently bad and our weaknesses. So if you've done something wrong and you end up in prison, it means that there is an aspect of your character that doesn't conform to society's norms. But importantly, there's an element within you that makes you behave in a certain way, an unloving way. The wise person is going to ask: *what caused me to behave in the way I did? What does that inform me about myself? Where do my weaknesses lie?* Being able to see and acknowledge the dark weaknesses within you makes you a complete person. You use these experiences to inform yourself about the contents of your subconscious. You're not a full person until you see, acknowledge and accept all aspects of your character. Both good and bad. Both painful and pleasurable. We're all guilty of trying to avoid what we perceive as weaknesses and negativity."

"And that's what people who suppress are doing?" I ask.

"Yes, most people are denying the existence of the negative aspect of their subconscious. If you supress something, it will eventually express itself in your material world."

"Which is exactly what happened to me in karate."

"Yes. And you start to judge and criticize other people who have the characteristic that you're suppressing."

"I noticed that in prison. Whenever anyone was accusing someone of doing something, it was nearly always the accuser who was doing it."

"That's right," Andrew says. "And they genuinely feel that it's somebody else. They're in denial of their own subconscious. For me, what's so exciting about the work I do is that I've realized with the use of meditation, introspection and discussion that we allow people to open up the subconscious, to access it, and to become complete people."

"Do you consider there is a risk to opening up the subconscious, a danger?"

"Not for the courageous," Andrew says.

"Everything in life has risk," I say.

"I had a dream experience in which I faced my apparent annihilation by demons. Falling down like that was a journey through my subconscious. At the end of the spiral was my true self. Although I was terrified beyond belief, I now know that if you make the complete journey you have nothing to fear."

"I had a similar dream myself months after I started taking crystal meth when I was a stockbroker. I dreamt that an invisible devil was coming to kill me. I was absolutely terrified. I woke up and looked around my bedroom, thanking the high heavens that it was only a dream. Then the devil came again. I was still in the dream. I kept waking up in the bedroom, thinking it was over. My terror got to the point where when I did finally wake up, I was paralyzed. I couldn't move or open my eyes. My eyelids were stuck. I had to strain to unglue them. It was one of the most frightening experiences of my life and it was all mental."

"I've come across accounts of saints," Andrew says. "When they begin their spiritual journey, they go through one of these processes. It's part of delving into the subconscious. In my case, negative energy was trying to frighten me off my spiritual journey, but in fact, the opposite happened. It allowed me access to who I really was. Ever since then, I've been gradually finding my own way down that spiral, working my way deeper and deeper into my subconscious, figuring out my fears. The reason why it shouldn't be dangerous is that you do it in stages with a proper teacher according to your ability and capacity, and it should unfold according to your strength and courage."

After chatting with Andrew for a few hours, I drive home with my brain brimming with his knowledge. Thanks to him, I've learned a lot about the karate incident. Every setback is an opportunity for self-development if we allow it to be. We must have the courage to look within ourselves even though we might not like what we see. Upon realizing that we all have good, bad, fear and anxiety inside of us, it's easier for us to accept and work on the negative. When we suffer an extreme setback, the more difficult it is for us to look inside, but the greater the opportunity for growth.

I like to think that I'm an open honest person in tune with my inner feelings, but I kept the incident with the drunks quiet for a quarter of a century. Repressed, it contributed to my anxiety. It bided its time to cause further harm, culminating with my hyperventilating. How I handled that situation is the opposite of how I dealt with incarceration. By writing about the jail conditions and sharing my descriptions, thoughts and feelings on the Internet, I was able to work through the negative impressions. Instead of repressing them, I minimized their harm. Jail was my biggest setback, but also my greatest opportunity for learning.

Lesson 6:
Cherish Life and
the Small Things

"There are only two ways to live your life.
One is as though nothing is a miracle.
The other is as though everything is a miracle."
– Albert Einstein

In 2001, I'm high on Ecstasy, GHB and assorted Mexican pharmaceuticals, moving at full throttle on a jet ski, skimming off the waves on the Sea of Cortez, Rocky Point and oblivious to how far I'm taking my partner Claudia away from land. Eventually the waves grow so big, I become alarmed and look over my shoulder. I'm shocked to see that the people on the beach are barely visible. They're the size of ants.

"Holy shit!" I say. "We'd better go back."

I try to turn the jet-ski. A wave the size of a bus capsizes us. Submerged below the jet-ski, I ingest salt water and panic. With the strength of ten people, the current drags me around underwater. Noticing the dark void towards the sea floor, I'm seized by fear of death and desperate for oxygen. Hoping to stop swirling, I thrash my limbs with maximum exertion and claw my way towards the light above the water. Managing to surface, I suck in air. Gasping, I spot Claudia, flailing her arms, struggling to keep her head above the water, her long blonde hair compressed to her face.

"Help!" she yells.

I swim towards her, but a massive wave throws us in different directions.

"Swim back to the jet-ski or else we're going to drown!" I yell.

"I can barely swim! I can't make it!"

"You have to!" I swim towards her.

"Oh my God! Are there sharks in here?" she shrieks.

Having no skills in water rescue, I reach and grab her body, but plunge us both underwater. To resurface, I have to release her. "Come on! We've got to swim to it before the next wave hits!"

Side by side, we swim to the jet-ski. We cling to it, panting.

"We've got to turn the jet-ski back up," I say. "Are you ready?"

"No."

"No?"

"I'm too weak."

"No, you're not! Come on. Try!" I yell, determined to convince her.

We wrestle with the heavy jet-ski. Every time we try to right it, the water slaps it back down. Exhausted, we have to keep taking rests, but eventually we turn it over. I grip Claudia's slippery body, shove her up and climb on. She hugs me from behind and we both slump forward, short of breath.

"Look how far away from land we are," she says, shivering.

"I don't know how to restart it. I've got this safety thing on my arm, but I'm so high, I didn't pay any attention to the emergency instructions."

"Me neither," she says, desperation in her big eyes.

"I'm such a dumb-arse," I say. "Maybe they'll see us from the beach and rescue us."

"What if we don't get rescued?" she asks. "What if we float further out to sea?"

"They'll realize something's up when we don't take the jet-ski back. They'll send someone out to look for us. We'll be alright, love," I say, unconvinced as we drift further away.

Soon, the people on the beach are imperceptible. We appear to be approaching a sea lane. Praying that we don't get run over by a ship, I hear a strange sound: *clippety-clippety-clippety*. Heading by us is a rickety wooden boat manned by wizened Mexican fishermen in blood-stained aprons. Two of them are carving up a massive fish and chucking chunks overboard as bait.

"Help! Help!" I yell.

As the boat drifts by, they squint at us as if experiencing a mirage. *Clippety-clippety-clippety...*

"Shit! They don't speak English!" Watching them leave, I panic. Drawing on the Spanish I know, trying to say, "Please help me. I don't understand how to start the jet-ski," I yell as if my life depends on it, "Señores por favor necesito su ayuda! Jet-ski, no entiendo! No entiendo! Por favor necesito su ayuda!"

The boat slows and starts to turn.

"Yes! They're going to help us. We're saved," I say, rejoicing.

As their boat nears, I notice they're scowling.

"Look at their knives," Claudia says, her eyes bulging with terror.

Reading her thoughts, it dawns that she could be raped or they could murder us. "Holy shit." Staring at the curved steel streaked with blood, I feel queasy.

One of them speaks in Spanish. They laugh, displaying rows of brown teeth, receding gums and gaps where teeth once resided.

I hold up the bracelet with the emergency jet-ski starter. "No entiendo!"

They laugh again. Their boat nudges the jet-ski. Taking me by surprise, the nearest grabs my arm with incredible strength. Startled, I tense my side to avoid falling into the sea. Leaning towards the jet-ski, the fisherman yanks the bracelet off my arm. He puts the key where it belongs and the engine starts. Although relieved, I'm alert for danger.

"Gracias, señores. Gracias," I say.

The fisherman who helped us steps aside. A fisherman with a sword-sized curved blade comes to the edge of the boat and lunges at me. Petrified, I almost jump into the water. Leaning, he puts the blade aside and spanks Claudia's behind. She shrieks. The fishermen cackle and laugh as if it's the funniest thing they've seen on the water for a while.

"Cheeky bugger!" I yell, outraged, but relieved that the jet-ski is working. "I think we've overstayed our welcome." I turn the jet-ski and speed away, thankful that we didn't drown or get sliced into bait by the fishermen.

Four years later in 2005, I'm no longer seeking thrills from dangerous activity. My temperament has plunged way back down to earth thanks to three years of incarceration. I'm doing a headstand on the recreation field at Buckeye prison, Arizona, when a ruckus snaps my concentration. Opening my eyes, I see the world upside down. Pumped-up tattooed prisoners of all races – wearing sunglasses and with Walkmans clipped to orange cut-off sports shorts – are abandoning their work-out regimens and flocking to the chain-link fence. To pay attention, I drop my legs down and stand up. They yell at a bespectacled man with slicked-back greying hair around 60 pushing his belongings across the yard in a creaky trolley escorted by a guard in a beige uniform.

"What's up, Two Tonys!"

"Two Tonys, wattup, dog!"

"How're you doing, old man?"

"They've finally let me out of the hole," Two Tonys says, smiling. "I'm coming to run this yard," Two Tonys says, joking. "Don't start no shit and there won't be no shit."

The audience laughs. Noticing his arrival, more people rush to the fence. The rapidly growing crowd shadows Two Tonys, ignoring the agitated guards with rifles patrolling the gun tower. After recreation, I tell my cellmate what I saw.

My cellmate says he's served time with Two Tonys. "He's a good dude. He's got a lot of stories about work he's put in for the old-school Mafia families. His associates all have funny names like Sal Spinelli and Harry the Horse."

"What's he in for?"

"Mass murder, but he says he never killed anyone who didn't have it coming. They were all rival gangsters. He's serving over 100 years."

My cellmate insists on arranging a game of chess be-tween me and Two Tonys. Although intimidated by his crimes, I win because he keeps speaking his mind and announcing his game plan. After I tell him why I won, he takes a liking to me for being honest. As I get to know him, the level of trust builds. He asks me to write his life story. Daily, he dictates his autobiography and I write it down.

He reveals secrets, including events surrounding unsolved murders. As we grow closer over the months, I start to feel like the son he never had. When an old member of the Aryan Brotherhood prison gang who's taken offence to my blogging issues a green light to have me smashed, chaos erupts on the yard. Some prisoners want to smash me. Others protect me. The crisis goes on for three days with me almost getting shanked. The prisoners protecting me include Two Tonys, who ultimately makes the situation go away by calling in a favour. Having murdered rival gangsters puts Two Tonys in the highest respect category in the prison hierarchy, so his decisions carry a lot of weight.

Having served decades, Two Tonys is a big reader. He introduces me to one of his favourite books: *One Day in the Life of Ivan Denisovich* by Alexander Solzhenitsyn. The protagonist in the novel, Ivan, is a political prisoner in a Soviet labour camp in the 1950's. The prisoners are worked to death in Siberia, where the temperature gets so cold that human spit freezes in mid-air. I'm gripped by the book. Reading about the misfortune of the Russian prisoners – some of whom freeze to death – puts my situation in perspective. Whenever things deteriorate on the yard, Two Tonys and I joke about how hard Ivan had it.

When beef is served for chow in our prison, Two Tonys says, "It might look like shoe leather and taste like shoe leather, but that's okay 'cause guess what? Ivan Denisovich would have snorted it up with his left nostril and been as happy as if he were having supper with the Russian president. That's my barometer now: how rough Ivan had it. Imagine being happy to lick some carrot gruel off a spoon. Or having to ride the cook's leg to come up on some extra gills and tails in your fish-eyeball soup. My point is this: how the hell can I complain when there's always someone worse off? Of course I'd like to be chowing down on a Caesar salad, some escargot, a little bowl of scungilli and some ravioli stuffed with spinach, but I ain't gonna let those thoughts get me down. At least we're not being worked to death in Stalin's gulags." Two Tonys smiles. "The other night, I was watching some TV show about the Norwegian explorer, Roald Amundsen. To get to the South Pole without dying he lived with the Eskimos for a few years, and learned how to live in harmony with that environment. That got me thinking: *prison is my environment.* I ain't going nowhere for the rest of my life, bro, except on a trip to the hospital every now and then. Instead of fighting my environment, I need to be living in harmony with it. I can't be raising my blood pressure because the breakfast biscuits were cold, or my cell door didn't open at exactly one forty-five for rec, or I didn't get called to Property when I was supposed to. I've got to go with the flow. Why should I be blowing gaskets over the small shit when there's people getting blown up in Iraq, mudslides are killing thousands in the Philippines, and there's earthquakes in Turkey? Shame on me."

After Two Tonys is transported to see an eye doctor, I ask him how it went.

"Have you ever been transported into Tucson from here?" Two Tonys asks.

"No."

"Let me tell you about the transportation guards: they're real negative. They're probably told, 'If you slip and fall, don't think a prisoner won't grab your gun and kill you.' They're trained to keep their distance and remain aloof. They're going to give us what we've got coming and no more: chains, transportation and a cup of water if there's a fountain around. They're not gonna talk about who won the ball game or where the nearest pizzeria is. They're real shitheads. Anyhow, I get to the doctor's office, and there must have been 20 people waiting to see him. I'm at the bottom of the list 'cause I'm a state prisoner. I look around and I got no one to talk to."

"How did the other patients react to you?" I ask.

"They wouldn't make eye contact with me. I've got belly chains on, ankle chains, I'm sitting between two guards packing Glock pistols, and they didn't wanna look at me. So I'm looking at them, studying them. There must have been six old couples. I start figuring stuff out in my brain 'cause I've got nothing better to do. I'm gonna be stuck there for a couple of hours staring at them.

"Here's what I see: a couple across from me about my age, probably married for 40 years. I see the guy in his grey knee-length shorts, his cotton shirt, his argyle socks and his Nike-swoosh shoes. You know, presentable. A typical retired suburbanite who probably got a gold watch when he quit working for the phone company or the insurance company or some other shit, where they gave him cake and donuts at the office cubicle party, and told him what a swell guy he'd been for the past 25 years, running from cubicle to cubicle, saying how much they were gonna miss him – till his ass hit the door. And the guy's just sitting there, looking at the wall. Not saying anything to the old prune-faced lady sitting next to him, who he's gotta be nice to, and will probably miss like hell when she dies. And she's just sitting there looking at the wall as well, and I said to myself, *You know what? He's doing time. You think this guy ain't doing time? He's gonna see the doctor, and she's gonna give him moral support after they squirt that shit in his eye.* After they squirted me, I couldn't see shit on the way home. I had to feel my way to the chow hall. *And then he's gonna go home to his nice middle-income house with a pool in the backyard, and the grandkids, who probably live in Cincinnati, are gonna come over and visit him once a year, at Xmas. And his old lady knows just how he likes his coffee in the morning.*

And they might or might not still be having sex – 40 years, come on now!

"Here's the crux of my thoughts: the old guy ain't no happier than me. I could see it in his face. I'm going back to prison, but I'm gonna clown with the youngsters and talk a lot of shit. I'll do a little walking and exercise. I'll enjoy my shows: *American Idol, Survivor*, and I watch a lot of Public Broadcasting Service. So what if I have to get up four or five times to pee during the night due to my enlarged prostate? The old guy ain't having as good a time as I am. He might have me on the food. He might be eating Waldorf salads and lamb cutlets with apple sauce or mint jelly, compared with my burrito mix and two tortillas. He's got me there. But I'm going to the store tomorrow. I'll get me some Milky Ways, Nutty Cones and a couple of Sprites. I'm gonna plug up my arteries real good, but I deserve a good time every now and then. I can tell you this much: the old guy may be eating better, but he ain't laughing harder. He ain't got the sense of adventure I'm having 'cause anything can kick off in the joint at any time and it often does. I ain't got it that bad. That's called PMA: my positive mental attitude, brother. Happiness is just a state of mind."

"I agree," I say. "But I'm still wondering what you were doing at the eye doctors?"

"He squirted some shit in my eye and looked at my cataracts to determine if he's gonna have to cut them out or not. This growing old business ain't for wimps. But you know what? A lot of guys don't make it. I'm sure you've heard of Achilles, the Greek warrior, a hero of the Trojan War who got whacked by Paris who hit him in the heel with a poison arrow?"

"Yes."

"Well, when Achilles was in hell, Odysseus asked him in so many words: is it better to die like a hero, young, in battle, or to grow old on your farm feeding your goats? Achilles reply was: I'll take the goat feeding or even be a slave any time."

Almost daily for a couple of years in prison, I have profound conversations about life, philosophy and literature with Two Tonys. His attitude is all the more impressive because he's never getting out and like most prisoners here, he has hepatitis C, which is slowly killing him because it's so difficult to get the prison to pay for treatment.

Shortly before my release, I arrange to meet Two Tonys to say goodbye.

Staring at my friend, I feel the sadness in his eyes. "You've taught me so much about putting things in perspective. Whatever life throws my way, I'm always going to ask, *How would Ivan view it?* I can't believe I'm never going to see you again."

"Me, too, little bro. But I'm sure glad we crossed paths on the road of life. Out of all the people I've ever met, you've changed my way of thinking the most."

"How so?" I ask.

"As well as all these books and discussions we've been having, you talk to everyone the same in here. You don't judge people."

"I really appreciate that coming from you. But ultimately *you've* changed your way of thinking."

"You need to take some freaking credit!" Two Tonys says, smiling. "And stop being so humble."

"Alright, I'm glad I've helped you," I say.

"That's more like it! I'm not good at saying good byes, so I'm gonna head back," he says, his voice quavering.

"Wait!" I yell, fighting back tears. Pressure runs down my jaw and rises up my face. "I love you, Two Tonys. I'm never going to forget you. I'm going to keep writing to you."

"I love you, too, my little bro." He stares, saying nothing, gazing intently, as if etching my image into his memory to take back to Yard 4 to cherish. He raises his hand and pats his heart. "L&R, little bro. L&R." In prison, L&R means love and respect. Behind his glasses, tears glisten.

Tears run down my face. "I'll always remember your PMA and what Ivan went through. L&R, Two Tonys."

Two Tonys was popular with the readers of my blog, Jon's Jail Journal. Sadly, his liver gave up and he died on September 8th, 2010. He wrote to me right up until the end. His death hit me hard. Blessed to have met him, I'm convinced that Two Tonys infused me with his spirit. Whenever I read the conversations of ours that I transcribed, I'm awe-struck by the profundity of his wisdom. He encouraged my writing and I still feel his presence with me, especially now as I type this chapter.

Before my arrest, I sought happiness in all of the wrong places, leading to danger and almost the loss of my life and Claudia's in Mexico. It took meeting people like Two Tonys for me to see the magic in the ordinary.

There are times when we react to small situations. On such occasions, thinking about Two Tonys' positive mental attitude helps me snap out of it. On the way to the fitness centre yesterday traffic was gridlocked. Stuck in their cars, unable to cope with the delay, some of the drivers appeared to be on the verge of giving themselves heart attacks. I arrived at the fitness centre to a line of people with long agitated faces. What were they worried about? Had the building received a bomb threat? No. Our BodyPump class was starting ten minutes late. Wondering what Two Tonys would make of the situation made me grin. Learning to put our difficulties into perspective prevents self-induced stress.

Incarceration and the philosophy of Two Tonys taught me to be at peace with reality. With no cockroaches in my bed, no dead rats in my food, no bleeding and itching skin infections and bed sores, I have little choice but to wake up with a smile.

Lesson 7:
Learn a Relaxation Technique

"If a man insisted always on being serious,
and never allowed himself a bit of fun and
relaxation, he would go mad or become
unstable without knowing it."
– Herodotus

In late 2002, my sister is concerned that I'm losing my sanity in the drug- and gang-infested Towers jail in Phoenix, Arizona. A practitioner of yoga, she mails me *Yoga Made Easy* by Howard Kent. Although grateful, I immediately hide the book under my mattress out of fear the prisoners will see it and brand me a sissy.

Over several weeks, the book gathers dust. In her letters, my sister keeps asking if I've tried yoga. My guilt at having not done so grows. *If I try the exercises one time and don't like them I can at least tell her I gave yoga a go.* I wait until my cellmates are downstairs and retrieve the book. On the grimy cement floor between the doorway and a toilet reeking of sewage, there's just enough space to do yoga. I try several basic postures to the best of my ability, bending this way and that and rotating my spine, worried that I'm going to pull a muscle in my stiff body. Holding the positions for up to one minute is harder than it looks in the book. Sweating in forward bend, I strain to touch my toes, but my fingers refuse to go any further than my shins.

At the end, thankful the routine is over and no one saw me doing it, I lie on my back in corpse pose and close my eyes. For the first time in jail, I feel all of the anxiety over my safety, the conditions and the uncertainty surrounding my case melt away. In particular, my shoulders are so re-laxed that all of the tension concentrated in that area and the back of my neck feels as if it's oozing out. I'm breathing slower and the constant worries have emptied from my mind. It feels so good, I stay there longer than the few minutes the book recommends, tuned into my heartbeat and out of the mayhem in the day room just a few feet away. *How's it possible to feel this good without drugs?* After yoga, I remain relaxed for a few hours until the worries and anxieties resume.

Being a sucker for things that feel great and craving more of the yoga fix, I abandon my inhibitions and start doing it daily. Fortunately, my cellmates spend most of their time in the day room watching TV or gambling at cards. Over the months, I advance to more difficult postures. At the end of each routine, I try to spend a few minutes meditating, but meditation doesn't make much sense. The book instructs me to sit cross-legged and to try and halt the flow of my thoughts, but every time the things in my head slow down, a thought intrudes and my brain speeds up again. I'm clueless about meditation, but the physical side of yoga is working so well for me, I resolve to persist with the mental.

Over several months, I make little progress with meditation. Having lived such a fast-paced life, one of the hardest parts for me is having the patience to sit for longer than a few minutes. Just when I'm managing to still my brain, a thought pops up about something pressing – I need to tell my lawyer this, I need to write to that person… – and before I know it my body is springing off the floor to handle what's on my mind. To keep such thoughts at bay, I pay attention to my breath by saying to myself, *in, out, in, out…* After a few minutes of using this technique, I stop monitoring my breath, and my mind goes quiet for a little bit at first, increasing over time.

In May 2003, when I'm transferred to the cockroach-infested maximum-security Madison Street jail, my stress level goes through the roof. I don't know anybody there, and most of my neighbours have committed serious crimes such as murder. Unable to sleep with the insects tickling my limbs, feet, and palms, not to mention them trying to burrow into my ears to eat my earwax – which I discover is like honey to them – I suffer a nervous breakdown. For several days, I hear imaginary voices threatening me harm. I start to see cockroaches that aren't there. Drops of water on the floor appear as cockroaches. Concerned for my mental health, I request to see a doctor. I'm prescribed medication to make me sleep. Grateful that the medication works, I fear getting addicted to the pills. The pills make me increasingly groggy and spaced out. I worry about the side effects. Hoping to get off the pills, I decide to gradually increase my meditation time from ten minutes to a few hours. So as not to be disturbed, I wait until the cells are locked-down. With my back parallel to a cement-block wall inhabited by cockroaches, I sit cross-legged and close my eyes.

At first, I'm intimidated by the prospect of calming my mind for longer than ten minutes. I start out concentrating on my breathing, counting breaths when I have to. Eventually, the thoughts stop. Every now and then a thought intrudes, but I refocus on my breathing. Thirty minutes in, I'm struggling to ignore aches and pains and pins and needles. I stop, but try again the next day. Over time, I learn to alternate crossed-leg positions to ease my discomfort. After an hour of meditating one night, my thoughts are barely there. I enter a deep state of relaxation as if all that exists is my breath, pulse and the movement of energy throughout my body. Sensing areas of tension within my face, I concentrate on allowing those subtle muscles to relax. My previously tense fingers open like flowers blooming. I want to meditate forever, but my cellmate using the toilet snaps me out of it. After meditating for a few hours every night for two weeks, I feel less stressed, so I stop the pills. My clarity of mind returns. I'm surprised at how easily I sleep after meditating. Some nights, I meditate for so long that images materialize in my brain.

At this crucial point of my life, meditation saves my sanity.

The supermaximum-security prison I go to after the jail houses the most dangerous prisoners in Arizona, including serial killers, the leaders of the main prison gangs such as the Arizona Aryan Brotherhood, and men awaiting execution on death row. Dressed in shank-proof body armour, including helmets with visors, the guards look like black cyborgs. In raised Plexiglas towers, the guards monitor several rows of locked cells.

My first cellmate is a Satanist with a pentagram tattooed on his forehead. Part of a cult that was sacrificing people, drinking blood and eating human body parts, he's in for murder. Fortunately, he's rather nice to me. He gives me a book on Leonardo da Vinci, which we discuss. Initially, I spend most of my time reading on my bunk. Three times a day, guards wheel a trolley laden with chow trays and feed us through a trap in the door. As my vegetarian diet hasn't yet been approved, I can barely eat. I'm allowed out of my cell once every three days to take a shower. To be extracted for a shower, I must strip naked in the cell, watched by a guard on the other side of the door. He yells commands and threatens to electrocute me with a Taser if he's disobeyed. In order for him to check all of my orifices for weapons, I must raise my arms, peel my ears forward, open my mouth, raise my tongue, lift my scrotum, pull my foreskin back and finally, turn around, bend over, stretch my behind wide open and cough. After the visual strip search, I put my white boxers and orange jumpsuit on and back up to the door. I'm handcuffed through the slot in the door. The door is opened and I'm escorted to the shower with the guard threatening to smash my skull into a wall if I don't maintain a straight line or if I look into any of the other cells or attempt to make any type of communication with my neighbours. Trudging along in cuffs, I pray that no prisoners I'm passing blast me with excrement and urine – a common method of attack in supermax prisons because the traditional method of settling disputes with fists isn't possible. The shower only runs for five minutes to prevent flooding, but I'm locked in the mouldy cubicle inhaling chlorine-tinged, humid air until a guard decides to escort me back, which can sometimes drag on for hours.

At nights, the lights are never turned off properly, there's a strange buzzing noise and translucent insects descend upon us.

In super-maximum security, there are nights when the inmates yell at each other into the small hours, making sleep impossible. I try to doze off with wet toilet paper shoved in my ears, but the noise penetrates right through. Rather than struggle against reality, I resolve to do yoga for as long as the people yell, which some nights lasts for several hours. If it wasn't for yoga, my body and spirit would be wasting away as I'm barely eating and I'm suffering moments of caged-animal despondency. My dad mails me a book on extreme yoga – a collection of Cirque du Soleil-style limb entwinements. My once stiff body starts bending into bizarre postures for hours, taking my mind off the environment. Over time, I feel as if I'm transcending the conditions rather than being crushed by them. Instead of standing frustrated for hours locked in the damp oppressive shower, peeping through the door hoping to attract the attention of guards who couldn't care less about letting me out, I start doing yoga in the shower – all postures that require standing up, including hula-hula, hip rotations that seem so preposterous in supermax that I can't help but laugh to myself and think, *If only the inmates or the guards could see me now.* Many a night when I'm upside down and twisted peculiarly in my cell, a guard halts his security walk, flashes a light on me and yells something like, "What in the goddam hell's going on in here?" Now, not only can I touch my toes in forward bend, I can grab my feet.

After four months of doing nightly yoga for hours on end, I'm moved to a medium-security prison. I'm still thin, but rock-like muscles are popping out of my arms and my thighs feel like steel cables are running through them. I have strength in places I've never felt it before. Inhibitions gone, I do yoga openly on the recreation field. Although some of the men stopping to stare are most certainly checking out my behind, others are impressed by my repertoire of strenuous postures, including upside-down ones. Some even request to join in.

During my final year of incarceration, some of the prisoners urge me to start a yoga class. I hold it in a bare dusty room with no mats, props or even air conditioning. Sweating non-stop, we lie on little towels and do headstands by resting the tops of our skulls on deck shoes. I entice my students by telling them that yoga isn't for sissies and that it confers certain advantages in prison such as having the flexibility to kick someone in the head. My students leave the class so relaxed that kicking heads is the last thing on their minds.

Released from prison in December 2007, I'm traumatized from living amid mayhem and violence for almost six years. I'm haunted by nightmares revolving around predators from prison hunting me down and trying to kill me. The local mental health team insist I take psychiatric medication to recover. The side effects include an inability to think clearly enough to write. To get off the medication, I accelerate my yoga and take up exercise such as Body-Combat. By the end of the year, I feel more normal. I'm still having nightmares, although not as intense.

Four years later in 2012, a friend invites me to two-days of Isha Yoga in London. Having no idea what I'm getting into, I agree to go because I trust her judgement. I end up in a massive room with 1000 people. The host, Sadhguru from India, has big brown kind eyes and an impressive white beard that frizzes out at the sides. He has a red shawl draped over traditional Indian clothing and an orange cloth wrapped around his head. During the morning meditation and breathing exercises on the second day, I flash back to jail. The experience runs through my mind like a film on fast forward, even including the visuals I saw when I meditated for hours on end in my cell back in the maximum-security jail. My face contorts uncontrollably as if I'm experiencing various emotional states in rapid succession. The tingling at the base of my spine builds into an intense warm feeling that slowly rises through my torso. Surprised by the ball of heat climbing my spine, I wonder what the hell's going on. As if a chain reaction has been set in motion, I'm powerless to stop it. The higher the ball rises, the more intense the heat and experience becomes. The vibrations running through my body are so strong that I rock back and forth in the hope of staying grounded. Rising from the back of my neck, the ball heats my head up. I feel a stream of powerful energy exit through the top of my skull. The chain reaction is over. Overwhelmed, surprized, I cry. I'm vividly aware that I just somehow released a chunk of my prison trauma. Even though I'm crying, I feel lighter and joyous. Other loud emotional reactions are happening all around me – screaming, shouting, laughing, giggling, sobbing. I sense that trauma is being released. Afterwards, we all radiate the same tranquillity and we express how unburdened we feel. When I get home, I post this to Facebook:

Just got home blissed out from two days of Isha Yoga at the ExCel Centre, London with 1000 yoga freaks and the hilarious yoga master Sadhguru Jaggi Vasudev who flew in from India. Sadhguru had people laughing, crying and at the end, dancing like wild moonies.

I actually left the building in the pouring rain, wearing only flip-flops, shorts and a T-shirt, with my arms in the air, getting soaked to the bone, yelling, "Mother Nature embrace me!" :) Must have looked like I was on drugs. :) Who needs drugs when you've got yoga? :)

In late 2012, I discover yin yoga. In a yin session postures are held from three to five minutes. Yin works on the deep tissues, releasing physical and emotional tension held within the body that has been accumulated over a lifetime. I leave my first yin session with every cell in my body rejoicing. Much to my surprise, the feeling lasts for several days. No matter what stressful events arise, I laugh them off.

Having tried many styles of yoga over a decade, I've found that yin is the best for me. As well as the yin sessions, I presently start each morning with 30 minutes of yoga, breathing exercises and meditation – a little routine that I learned at the Isha yoga weekend. It sets me up for the day. When I don't find the time for it, my body craves it.

Over the years, I've discovered that there's much more to yoga than dozens of women in leotards, stretching in a studio. Yoga is a system of many parts developed over thousands of years for psychological well-being, not just physical development. Besides exercises, yoga provides ways to train the mind and meditation is one of the most powerful. My mum, who suffers from depression, uses Vipassana meditation. It starts with ten days of complete silence and ten hours each day sat cross-legged meditating. When Vipassana was introduced to a high-security prison in the Donaldson Correctional Facility near Bessemer, Alabama tremendous transformation occurred in a variety of prisoners, including murderers. There is a documentary film about this called *The Dhamma Brothers*.

When I suggest yoga to people who are suffering mentally or physically, the two biggest objections I hear are, "I'm not flexible," and "I don't have the time to do it." When I started yoga, I wasn't flexible either. Flexibility is a benefit of yoga. Being a workaholic, I understand how problematic finding the time is. The umbilical cord between me and my computer is strong enough to moor a boat. But there came a point in my life when I made health and well-being a priority. If I hadn't made that decision, I'd never have found the time for yoga.

Without prison, I probably wouldn't have learned a relaxation technique. For me it was yoga, but for you it may be a Jacuzzi, a massage or a different type of exercise.

One thing is certain though: people who perform the best in life use at least one relaxation technique. The regular employment of such a technique actually changes how the brain reacts to stress. We become less prone to emotional outbursts and the reactions that we do have are shorter. Relaxation techniques counteract the unhealthy chemicals our brains release during stress, boost our immune systems and we live happier and longer.

Lesson 8:
Let Go of Fear and Anxiety

*"Nothing in life is to be feared, it is only
to be understood. Now is the time to understand
more, so that we may fear less."*
– Marie Curie

In 1984, I'm a shy student. Anxious thoughts sometimes keep me awake at night. I go to pubs and clubs with my teenage friends, but I don't talk to anyone other than them. I never approach girls. I'm too self-conscious to dance. Alcohol doesn't impress me either.

Five years later when raving begins in the UK, I take Ecstasy in Manchester at a club called the Thunderdome. My anxiety melts. All I feel is euphoria. On the drug, I can't stop dancing, smiling and hugging complete strangers. I make friends with half of the club, opening up to them as if we've known each other all of our lives. By the end of the night, I'm dancing on the main stage facing a sea of ravers, having the time of my life. On weekend nights when my hometown friends refuse to go raving, I set off for Manchester on my own, confident that I'll have people to talk to and that I'll be invited to after-parties. I start dressing in bright colours. I take a sparkly silver cowboy hat to wear on the stage. My behaviour attracts attention from girls who invite me back to their places. On Ecstasy, I'm a different person. Studying on the weekdays, all I look forward to is raving.

Seven years later at the start of my Ecstasy dealing, it's my involvement in the drug community that results in me forming an alliance with the one of the most powerful criminal organizations in Arizona: the New Mexican Mafia. A product of the prison system, the New Mexican Mafia tends to murder anyone who gets in their way, including rivals, informants and prison guards. They even sanction a hit on the director of the state prison system. Our relationship forms almost accidentally. In the beginning, I don't know who they are or the danger I'm putting myself in.

One night in 1997, I'm at an apartment party in Tempe with mostly students. A young policeman walks in claiming he smelled marijuana from outside. He orders us not to move or leave. The supplier of the marijuana, a tall Mexican American with a tough handsome face called G Dog, pulls a gun on the policeman, and yells, "You don't move! The only one who's not leaving here is you! Everyone else get outta here!" We escape into the night. Minutes later, there's banging on the French windows of the students' apartment I'm hiding at. It's G Dog. We let him. The police search the complex with dogs and a helicopter. I'm terrified of getting caught but the danger passes. G Dog tells me that for helping him, not only does he have my back but so do his people. I'm unsure what he means.

Weeks later, he takes me to meet his brother. One of the first things I notice in Raul's house is a rocket-propelled grenade launcher on top of a giant TV. It dawns that Raul is into different criminal activity than me, but I still don't know that the house is a hub for the New Mexican Mafia. In the kitchen are bulk cocaine, crystal meth and various weighing scales. In a closet, Raul is growing hydroponic marijuana. I start to supply Raul with Ecstasy.

Over the months, I sometimes go to Raul's two or three times a week. The atmosphere is always tense. Most of his customers are wide-eyed meth users. His associates are massive tattooed Mexican Americans armed with a variety of guns. Raul always takes care of business with me efficiently, so he can move onto his next visitor. Thankfully, I never stay long.

One afternoon, I arrive to Raul with five associates, heads shaved, their bodies tattooed with flames, skulls, roses and the MM in a circular patch (which years later in prison, I learn means Mexican Mafia).. Usually, they eye me suspiciously, but now they're gazing as if they want me dead. My stomach drops. *Something's wrong.* Hearing the door behind me lock, I turn to an associate brandishing an MP5, a sub-machine gun that looks like a shortened rifle with a clip of bullets attached underneath. *There's no way out!* I hope my baggie clothes conceal how much I'm trembling. Too scared to speak, I glance at Raul, my eyes appealing for an explanation.

"Remember what I told you about never speaking to cops?" Raul asks.

Their focus on me intensifies. The sense that my answer is going to determine my fate almost paralyzes me. I slur my words: "Yeah. If I get pulled over and they ask to search my car without probable cause, I have the right to refuse. I don't need to tell them anything, but you said it's Okay to say that I came here looking for G Dog. If they do arrest me, I tell them that I want a lawyer. The lawyer you recommend is Alan Simpson."

Raul nods as if satisfied with my explanation, but maintains his interrogative expression. "What did you say to them when they pulled you over coming from here?" he asks, brow furrowed, hazel eyes ablaze, head cocked back. His associates remain quiet and fixated on my body language.

The sense of the danger I'm in rises. *They kill people who speak to the cops. Why do they think I've spoken to the cops? How can I convince them I've not?* My pulse magnifies, making my entire body feel as if it's throbbing and expanding. "I've never been pulled over coming from here," I say with an edge of protest.

"That's not what we were told."

"Whoever told you that is full of shit," I say forcefully, hoping to convince them.

"Someone gave a police report."

"Who said it was me? Does the police report have my name on it?" I ask, clenching my brow.

"Shut up and stand still!" In a white wife-beater vest and shin-length denim shorts, a man as broad as an ox steps forward with an iron bar, his eyes so big and crazy it's impossible for me to hold his gaze.

Assuming he's going to knock me out, so they can take me out to the desert, I jump out of his way. Two of them grab me. In a panic, I squirm.

"We're not gonna hurt you, homey," Raul says. "We just wanna know the truth."

"Okay," I say. "I'm telling the truth. I'll do anything you want to prove it."

The two pin me to a wall. The biggest approaches. He holds up the bar. I notice it's not an iron bar. It's an electronic device. He wands it over me. It beeps near my belt buckle.

"You're gonna have to strip down," Raul says.

"Okay," I say, guessing that they're trying to detect a police wire.

Embarrassed but more concerned about my safety, I disrobe. Naked, I reveal a trembling body streaked with sweat. One of them searches my clothes. The wand runs over my clothes, but it only beeps at my belt buckle.

"Put your shit back on," Raul says.

"We was told you got pulled over and gave a police report," Raul says, his voice less harsh.

I scan the other associates. None of their expressions have softened.

"That never happened. I'd have told you or G-Dog right away," I say, dropping his brother's name to remind him of our relationship.

"We're gonna grill the other person and find out what's going on. It's all good, homey."

Shook up, I leave afraid to drive in case the police are around, yet keen to get as far away as possible. At home, I take Valium to calm down.

Later on, I find out from G Dog that the person who implicated me had been pulled over and gave a police report. That person disappears.

A few years later, Raul and some of the men I knew from his house make headline news, charged with numerous murders and murder for hire. I'm shocked to learn they're part of the New Mexican Mafia. News of my association with them spreads throughout the rave scene, enhancing my reputation in the drug community.

Until the SWAT team smash my door down, I live a double life of club drugs versus study and work. Whenever my anxiety rises or I need to deal with scary people such as the New Mexican Mafia or Sammy the Bull's crew, I take more drugs. Out of my natural state, I'm the life of the party. But in jail, I'm sober and forced to live with violent intimidating people. For the first few days in jail, I can't sleep. Gang members and drug-craving psychopaths roaming for victims are generating constant violence. I have to get used to the sound of heads getting smashed against toilets, bodies being thrown around and people getting extracted on stretchers who look like they're dead. My anxiety is such that my heart beats frantically all night long, keeping me awake.

Early on, I'm warned that my nervous body language is an invitation to be raped, robbed or assaulted. I have no choice but to toughen up or face the consequences. For the first time in my life, I can't afford to have anxiety. Over the years, dealing with certain prisoners helps strengthen my resolve. They include my cellmate, Bud, whose welcoming statement is, "I've got a padlock in a sock. I can smash your brains in while you're asleep. I can kill you whenever I want." Bud was breaking into houses and taking a hammer to the kneecaps of his victims. We don't get along. He has a massive biker assault me just when I'm on the way to a Christmas visit with my parents. After that, Two Tonys takes me under his wing, protecting me from the biker and other threats.

In prison, gang rules dictate that people stick with their own race, so I'm taken by surprise when an almost 6½ foot African American shows up at my cell door, his physique so big that the inmates call him John Coffey after the innocent prisoner on death row in the movie *The Green Mile*. I stare at him cautiously, nervously, wondering what he wants. He introduces himself as T-Bone. He's served almost two decades. He wants to chat about the history of England. I ask him about the massive scars covering his body. Every single one is from a separate life-and-death prison fight. But not only is he standing up for himself, he's using formidable fighting skills acquired as a US Marine to

94

stop prison rape. It's not as simple as knocking the rapists out either. They stabbed him and tried to crack his skull open with river rocks. There were times when he felt his life ebbing away, but he managed to remain conscious and defeat his opponents. He credits his belief in God for giving him the strength to soldier on. I start to post his stories to the Internet and we become friends. When a hillbilly with a shank threatens to rape me while eating my commissary, T-Bone knocks the hillbilly out. He also protects me in other situations. He jokes that I'm going to be an author some day and he'll be my bodyguard. He tells me numerous stories about fighting prison rapists, including this one:

"Three youngsters were bulldogging a guy who wasn't into the game so to speak. I walked by and told the guy, 'Stand up for yourself or they'll never stop because you've already been punked!' The guy started to walk behind me, and people were saying he was my punk behind my back. He asked his wife and mother to send me money. I laughed and told him to stand up for himself. All the guys in my crew told me there was going to be a problem and that I was on my own because I couldn't protect every stray that came along. I said the guy only needs some guidance. They said people were saying I am soft. I didn't care because life is what we make it.

"A few weeks went by and then – bam! – I was hit upside the head by a youngster, Badu, a hardcore gang leader from LA. Badu was 6' 2", 270 pounds or more and fast. For murder, he was doing life with no parole, so that gave him an advantage over me because he had nothing to lose. He said I was taking his punk and I had better back off and find someone else to have sex with! Man, my head was on fire. The smell of my own blood came to me. I couldn't see straight. Things were all out of sorts and I couldn't focus.

I could have been killed. That's how I know that there is a Higher Power.

"Anyways, I dug deep within myself and got to my feet and saw the rock in Badu's hand. He was on his way into the little man's room and he was yelling at the guy to get ready to give him sex raw. All the cells were closing and I stuck my head in the shower and felt the lump on the side of my head – real close to my temple. I was thinking he tried to kill me. There wasn't anything else for me to do but get busy.

"I pulled off my shirt and wiped my face and head and ran to the cell. Badu was raping the guy again. Badu's cellmate had his head towards the wall, too scared to help the guy. Things went quick after that! I was hit in the right shoulder by the rock because I used a shoulder roll to defend myself. This part might sound nasty, but Badu wouldn't even stop raping the guy. I grabbed his left arm, pushed him towards the wall and he got me good. The sicko kicked me in the thigh and I was about to go down out of reflex because it hurt. I mean it really hurt. He took his eyes off my chest and tried it again and – bang! – I hit him with a left cross in his eye and then a right foot to his sternum. I followed up with the best punch I've ever hit any man with. He just dropped and that was it. I looked at him and I was out of it. I mean really seriously out of it. I sat on his chest and grabbed his neck and pounded his head on the floor! I wanted to kill that sick piece of human waste but something touched my heart. I got off him and the cops were standing there with their mouths open because they let that piece of shit do whatever he wanted because he ran a gang from LA to Arizona. The rape victim was crying.

"I was praying at Medical and the guards said, 'Go back to your cell! Seventy-two hours lockdown!' That's all they did. That was it.

"The rape victim stood up for himself after that. He lost all of his battles, but he learned to show heart. Badu became quiet and lost everything. So you've got to stand for something or you'll fall for anything!"

Time after time, T-Bone demonstrated the opposite of fear and anxiety: courage and composure. When I review the injuries I've had over the years they seem insignificant in comparison to T-Bone's fights. It puts my anxiety over karate sparring into perspective. In karate we wear mitts and pads and anyone who draws blood is immediately disqualified. T-Bone risked his life for complete strangers armed with rocks and knives. In prison and the Marines, there were times when he had no choice but to fight to the death.

Over regular lunches at The Beano, a local café, I try to learn as much as possible from my meditation teacher.

"I remember your class on fear and anxiety," I say. "You said that most of us fear things that are never going to happen or we are anxious about things that have happened in the past that we can't change."

"Let's start out on a basic principle," Andrew says. "The effect of the ego is to create duality."

"What do you mean by create duality?"

"You are at your core a spark of nature. Nature is like the sea and the ego is like a drop of water that wishes to remain separate from the sea. When a drop of water enters the ocean, it doesn't stop being a drop of water, but it does become part of the whole ocean and connects with everything. In our natural state, we are connected to everything, but the ego doesn't like that. It wants to remain separate. How does the ego remain separate? It has various mechanisms. If you remain in the present moment, you remain connected to everything. One of the mechanisms the ego uses to ensure you are detached from universality is fear. To do so it takes you out of the present and instead creates a false universe."

"So when I see myself dying in a plane crash or getting eaten by sharks or my skull getting fractured in karate, they're all false universes?" I ask.

"Yes. Your ego has created scenarios, which are pure fiction. By creating fiction, your ego ensures that you remain detached from your true self. You're detached from achieving anything out of fear that something will happen. A good example is if you take a child into a garden and show the child all of the beautiful plants. Imagine that the child acknowledges all of the beauty that exists and then gets stung by a nettle. The child now knows to avoid the nettle. Now if you take the child into a garden and introduce it to the nettle first, and the child gets stung, the child will think that everything that's green is painful, and have unnecessary fear and anxiety. Now, we are grown people. If you're brought up in a really unpleasant environment, then you're more likely to fear relationships because your first relationship was negative. Also, if someone is in a relationship and they get hurt, the ego will say avoid relationships because it loves to take any opportunity it can to manipulate you. That's how fear detaches people from people."

"But aren't fear and anxiety necessary for us to perform certain tasks?" I ask.

"Yes. If you think about going into a garden and getting stung by a nettle, you realize that you should avoid nettles – but not everything green."

I laugh.

"The same applies with being careful crossing the street to avoid getting run over," Andrew says.

"It seems that the creation of false scenarios in my mind is the bottom line when it comes to my fear and anxiety. I do it all the time. I guess I've got to keep reminding myself what's really going on."

"The other thing is that you're constantly following patterns of thought inherited from your parents, the people you interacted with at school and anyone else who had an influence over you. Most of those people were not living in the present moment. In order to form relationships with your parents and siblings, you emulated them. You wanted to be like them, so they accepted you. Right from the time you were in the womb, you were picking up the thought patterns of your mother and you started replicating them. From an early age, you thought it was the right way to behave and it became habitual."

"That doesn't bode well for me then as my mum has a tendency towards anxiety and depression," I say.

"It takes wisdom and true teaching to make you realize that everything about your upbringing in relation to those influences and everything in society are all manipulating your fears and anxiety. For example, the marketing industry understands the ego perfectly well because they are always manipulating you with that knowledge."

"That's one of the reasons I don't watch much TV."

"I haven't had a TV in my house for 15 years," Andrew says.

"Whenever I'm at my parents' and they turn on the news, it's always murder, mayhem and disaster."

"Yet stand in any street," Andrew says, "in the western world, and you see none of that. You see consideration, kindness, people being pleasant, everyone getting along. But the news will report that someone somewhere in the UK was killed. Yet, 60 million people living harmoniously isn't news."

I laugh. "What about fear, anxiety and comfort zones?"

"There are certain things we humans have to acknowledge and accept. One is that there will be pleasure and pain. We're happy to accept the pleasure."

"I know all about that," I say, smiling.

"But we don't wish to acknowledge that there's going to be pain. In order for there to be personal growth, there has to be some degree of pain, whether it be emotional, psychological or whatever. If you're going to expand as a person, you've got to be able to move outside of the world of the ego: the things you are attached to, your desires, your hopes. The ego offers you the security of ignorance, and yet our evolution requires us to move out of the small world of the ego and become universal. It's the impulse to become universal that takes you out of your comfort zone. In order to come out of your comfort zone, you have to take on your fears. You fear that if you give up something like security, then you're going to move into the void of the unknowing. As you move into that void, you have to let go of the things that are familiar to you. To expand as a person, you have to let go of the security and trap of the ego."

"Can you give an example of that?"

"I had a very secure job once, but I wanted to expand. I knew if I took on a different type of job it would take me to expansion, but I'd have to give up the security of the old job. Another example is if you're in a toxic relationship with someone and you know it's damaging you, you often stay in that relationship because you don't want to move into the void of the unknowing; you remain with something that's known. It's only by moving into the void that you're ever going to find out what's out there. It's fear. Your ego tells you, *Oh, if you give up this relationship there's no one out there for you. All the good ones are taken. You'll be alone.*"

"With my first wife, Sumiko, who attacked me, I always

thought things were going to improve. For years, I clung onto the hope that things would get better rather than take the risk of getting out. Things got worse. Once I went into the void and looked back, I wondered why I hadn't gone into the void much earlier."

"I'm told that if you go into a relationship hoping to change someone, you're a fool. And I'm just as guilty as anyone else," Andrew says.

"I feel like a fool for staying with Sumiko for so long."

"So you know you're in a toxic relationship," Andrew says, "you know you should get out of it, you fear being alone, and the reason you fear being alone is that you'll have to face your subconscious. In the absence of stimulation from the outside, you may have to face the contents of your subconscious, which are your fears and anxieties."

"As usual, I had to learn the hard way about overcoming my fear of exiting toxic relationships."

"No suffering, no spiritual growth," Andrew says, smiling.

Afterwards, I walk home from The Beano feeling free of fear and anxiety, but I know that my fears and anxieties will creep back in. I resolve to remind myself that the things I fear are mostly false universes created by my own mind.

The worst part about jail was being un-sentenced because my mind lived in a false universe in which I received a life sentence and never got out of prison. I couldn't get that thought out of my head. I tortured myself with it for 26 months. Meditation and yoga helped, but if I had known what I was doing to myself as explained so eloquently by Andrew, I would have saved myself tonnes of stress. Getting sentenced to 9 ½ years was one of the happiest days of my life because it freed me from the false universe. I knew exactly when I would get my freedom back.

The year following my release from prison is a bit of a blur, but I remember the fear and anxiety associated with the adjustment process. As well as my incarceration, I'd been out of the UK for almost two decades, so there was reverse culture shock. But once I'd adjusted, most of the fear and anxiety I'd felt throughout my life that drove me to drugs wasn't there. Having to deal with extremely dangerous people ranging from the New Mexican Mafia to prisoners I didn't get along with gave me a skill set. Being forced to live, day in day out, with hundreds of prisoners, crushed a lot of the shyness and anxiety out of me.

Zipping through life avoiding my fears and taking drugs to deal with them exacerbated my problems. I finally gained control of my life after I was forced to confront what I'd avoided. Now I know to expose myself to my fears and to not fear things that will never actually happen – all of the false scenarios my mind generates.

Lesson 9:
Learn to Love the
Right Person

*"Love is a fire. But whether it is going
to warm your hearth or burn down your
house, you can never tell."*
– Joan Crawford

In 1993, I arrive home anticipating an enjoyable evening with Sumiko, my Japanese wife. As I put my briefcase down, she charges from the living room. "Why you home so late? You having sex with a blonde woman?" she asks, shoving me.

Standing at the foot of the stairs in our plush home, I flash back to her previous outbursts. *How can this be happening again?* I raise my arms to block her strikes. "No. Calm down. Why're you so angry?"

"Why every guy like blondes so much?" She swears in Japanese.

"Come on, don't –"

"You like having sex with a blonde woman?"

"I called you from the office and you called me, so you know I couldn't possibly have been out with any blonde woman. Did you take your Zoloft today?"

"I throw away medication."

"What! Why?"

"It makes me sick. I sleep too much. I know you having sex with a blonde woman."

For half an hour, I repeat the same reassurances. Sumiko eventually collapses onto the sofa and sobs. I go upstairs to shower. The hot water relaxes my neck and shoulders. My thoughts and breathing slow down. Soaping my armpits, I ponder how to convince her to resume taking Zoloft. I'm lost in thought when the shower curtain rips open. I jump.

"Why you having sex with a blonde woman?" Sumiko screams, thrusting a Ginsu knife at my penis, her face crazed.

I flick my pelvis back, only just avoiding the blade. "Put the knife down!" I yell, my heart pumping violently.

"You having sex with an American woman, I cut off your penis." She lunges at me, arcing the knife at an angle that would slice my penis off like a sausage.

I try to leap back, but my head and rear slam into the shower wall. The knife misses my penis, but swoops again. With no distance to put between myself and the knife, I risk my hand to save my man parts. My arm lashes out. A finger burns as if in contact with the hot metal. I wince. The pain and sight of blood coming from my sliced-open finger send strength through me. I snatch her wrist. "Drop the knife!"

She struggles to hold onto the knife. Blood droplets expand on the shower floor and swirl down the drain.

"Drop the knife!" I yell, strengthening my grip.

The blunt end of the knife stubs my toe. "Ow!"

The muscles creasing up her angry face reverse direction into gloom. She bawls, softening my mood.

Blaming her mental illness, I hug her. "It's okay. Everything's going to be okay."

Over the following days, her mental health deteriorates. Whenever I suggest taking Zoloft, she grows hysterical. She smashes plates and hurls the iron around, making holes in the walls. Nothing I say calms her down. To avoid her, I work longer hours.

One night after an outburst, I go to bed with a chest of drawers against the bedroom door to keep her out. In the middle of the night, the sound of her stabbing the door wakes me up. Assuming my barricade is impenetrable, I stick in some earplugs and doze off. Hours later, movement in the room wakes me up. I spot a figure looming over me about to drop a small TV on my head. I jerk off the bed like a lizard and fall onto the carpet. The TV bounces off the mattress. Mystified as to how Sumiko entered, I turn the lights on. Above the chest of drawers is an oval-shaped hole she crawled through. She accuses me of having sex with a blonde friend of hers.

"Don't be silly!" I say. "If I'm going to work tomorrow, I need to sleep!"

She explodes and bites my bicep.

"Ah! That hurts! Get off my arm! Let go!" I flap my arm.

She clamps down harder, like a dog refusing to let go of a stick. She grimaces at me, her bloodshot eyes frantic, unblinking, animal-like. Blood streaks down her chin. I step away. Still attached, she drags along, intensifying my pain. I try to turn around, but her teeth are locked. The more aggressively I shake my arm, the tighter she bites, and the more it hurts. I want to punch her head, but I was raised never to hit a woman. I don't know what to do.

"Look, if you don't let go, I'm going to run at the wall and we're both going to get hurt. This is your last chance."

When it starts to feel as if hot needles are sticking into my arm, I clench my teeth and ram us into the wall. Bang. Jolt. *Ow!* My body bounces. My legs almost go out. Stunned, I reel, but manage to steady myself.

Knocked off balance, Sumiko falls onto all fours. She cranes her neck, revealing a blood-smeared face. She snarls and positions as if about to pounce up. Noticing that my arm appears to have grown a mouth, I go light-headed. The sight of the wound sobers Sumiko up. Yelling sorry, she runs for a first-aid kit. She cleans the wound, applies ointment and bandages it up. It needs stitches, but I don't fancy explaining myself to hospital staff. Sumiko sobs and swears never to be violent again. Committed to marriage and believing her, I decide to give her one more chance.

Months later on a Sunday afternoon, Sumiko storms into our home, denies she's been at a hotel having sex with a lover on Saturday night even though I suspect she has and accuses me of cheating. "You have sex with a blonde last night! How could you do this to me, Shaun? I know you having sex with a blonde woman. Come here, let me smell your penis." Sumiko leaps at my zipper, nose first, attempting to detect the smell of sex, her arms outstretched, claws curled, like a cat trying to snatch a bird.

I jump backwards and run to the far side of the coffee table. "I've not been having sex with any blondes and I'm so sick of you saying this crap! You're the one who stayed out all night and not at the house you told me you were staying at!" I'm weary of patching things up, only to suffer further outbursts. *I'm not spending the rest of my life dodging plates, worrying about the fate of my penis...* At my wit's end, my belief in staying married forever no matter what is finally over.

Giving chase, Sumiko yells, "Why you run? Why you no let me smell your penis? I knew it! Let me smell your penis!"

"Piss off!"

Sumiko stops. She hits her face repeatedly. *Slap-slap-slap...* When she stops, her porcelain skin is pink. She disintegrates into sobbing. "I knew it, you having sex with a blonde. That's why you no let me smell your penis," she says, crying like a little girl who has fallen off a bicycle.

Pitying her, I want to give her a hug. I move forward a bit, but just as quickly draw back, prevaricating, wary of entering her striking zone. Reminding myself she cheated, I feel disgust.

She drops her hands. Her features contort. Her frown lines deepen. Her eyes haze over in a distant and disturbed way as if bearing witness to her own brain falling apart. "You having sex with a blonde woman!" She pounces again, lashing out with her claws. "Why you no let me smell your penis? I get you! Come here; let me smell your penis!"

Weary of doing laps around the coffee table, I fly up the stairs like an Olympian and barricade the bedroom door. Hearing glass shattering in the kitchen, I call the police and wait. I emerge to two policemen inspecting the carnage.

In a timid voice, Sumiko tries to placate them, but I can tell she's seething inside. Shaking their heads, they see through her.

Perhaps her craziness is an act.

"You're to spend the night at a friend's house. If you come back to this house, you will be arrested. You will go to jail. We're sick of having to deal with you. There are more important things we could be doing with our time. Do you understand me?"

"Yes," Sumiko says.

"Do you think you can stay away from this house for tonight?"

"Yes. I stay friend's house."

The police give her a ride.

Figuring Sumiko will return tomorrow, repentant, eager to clean up the glass, I throw pillows on the sofa and try to rest. I watch stock-market news for at least an hour.

I hear a key opening the front door. On alert, my body tenses. Sumiko charges in. She rushes to the kitchen to arm herself. I dash upstairs, dodging plates and dial 911.

When the commotion stops, I creep down the stairs, hoping she's gone, yet watchful for a plate attack. "The police are on their way," I say, trying to flush her out. "Sumiko, I know you're in the kitchen." No response. Feeling a bit safer, I enter the kitchen. No sign of her.

From behind a kitchen counter, Sumiko springs up as if on a trampoline, wielding the iron and an expression of savage concentration. Yelling in Japanese, she chases me.

I run for the stairs, craning my neck in case the iron is launched. At the foot of the stairs, I watch her let it go, aiming it ahead of me, so that I'll run into it. I stop.

The iron arcs up, its cord in tow like a comet's tail. It ploughs into the grand chandelier. So many shards rain down, the ceiling appears to cave in. We gape. Glass bounces everywhere. Off the walls. The cabinets. The tabletop. The chairs. Us. The iron hits the floor. The room falls silent.

The police arrive and arrest Sumiko. I move out.

My first marriage is over.

A few years later in prison, Dr. Owen asks, "Have you been married?"

"Yes, three times. Twice legally and one was an exchange of blood."

His eyes widen.

I continue: "My first wife was a Japanese millionairess almost ten years older than me. When we met, I hadn't long been in America. I was impressed by her cooking skills, opulent apartment and Cheung piano. We'd only known each other for six months when we got married. As soon as the ring was put on her finger, her dark side emerged."

"Why did you marry so quickly?"

"She said she'd be more secure in our relationship if we got married. I said yes to please her even though it was too soon. I lacked emotional maturity. The stress she put me through attacking me and demolishing our house time after time was one of the reasons I started doing crystal meth. During the other two marriages, I was on drugs. The next, the blood exchange, was a former model turned gangster."

In the early nineties, walking down Scottsdale Road high on Ecstasy, I met Kelly, a black former Calvin Klein model who packed a Derringer handgun. Both of us were fans of house music. We hit it off. Foolishly, I started taking crystal meth with her. In 1995, we decided to marry, but not in a legal sense. A collector of serial-killer books, Kelly was a fan of the wedding scene in the movie *Natural Born Killers*, in which Mickey Knox slashes his palm and the palm of Mallory and they smudge their palms together in a blood oath. In a forest near Sedona, Kelly produced a blade and slashed our fingers. High on meth, we comingled our blood. We stayed together for three years. As she didn't approve of my Ecstasy dealing, we separated on good terms.

"Shortly after we met, Kelly wanted to move her waterbed. Unable to drain it, she pulled a gun out and shot it. One time when she was high on meth and hadn't slept for a week, she almost shot a man in the back at a rave that she thought had threatened her, but it was a case of mistaken identity. I was so high back then, her carrying a gun excited me. My third wife, Amy, was a University of Arizona student, but also a strip-tease dancer and big-time party animal. We managed to live a crazy lifestyle for a while, but we sowed the seeds of each other's destruction."

In 1999 – when my wealth, drug consumption, Ecstasy ring and insane behaviour were all at a peak – I married Amy at the Little White Chapel on the Las Vegas Strip. Besides studying chemistry, Amy was doing lesbian Internet porn. She sometimes invited girlfriends to share our bed. Things turned ugly after Amy returned from Mexico claiming she was raped. When I learned that the rape was a cover story for her infidelity, my heart broke. I went on a drug rampage that lasted for weeks. The stock market crashed, and as I wasn't watching it, I lost most of my wealth.

"Looking back on my life, most of my craziest behaviour and stupidest choices revolved around my relations with women. Before my arrest, I finally met Claudia, the golden hearted woman of my dreams. But the SWAT team smashed our door down. She stayed with me for almost two years after my arrest, but the strain of having a boyfriend in jail was too much for her. I ended up single thanks to the years of disastrous choices I made."

"You need to be able to analyse your relationships. If you don't factor in your previous mistakes, you'll repeat them. How did you analyse stocks?"

"I'd analyse data: moving-averages of price, volume, that kind of stuff," I say excitedly. "I'd review thousands of charts, read annual reports, especially the notes, look at various financial ratios and come up with a short list of stocks I felt had a high probability of success."

"When you were running the math, how did you feel?"

"I had tunnel vision. Nothing else existed. That worked well. I got rich, but I self-destructed."

"That's why you have to look at the reasons, understand the road map, watch for the danger signals - blinking lights, cabarets, dancing girls, whatever. Most guys think with their little head. Do you have a penchant for that?"

"I did in the past."

"In relationships in general, you need to apply the analytical discipline you apply to stock selection. Here's what I'm seeing: with yoga, you're doing well with your spiritual side; with stocks, your pragmatic side seems fine. It's the emotional side you're having problems with."

"I do have a deficit there. My mum and sister want to put their seal of approval on future girlfriends. In the past, I've chosen the wrong partners and during breakups, my depressions and drug-taking increased. I never realized I should step back and analyse potential partners with the discipline I analyse stocks. That's an important point you've made."

"When it comes to relationships, you've got your ratios all wrong."

Before my release, T-Bone offers me some advice. "Something you really need to do is sit down with Mom and Pop and learn who they really are as human beings. How long have they been married?"

"Nearly 40 years."

"Can you imagine all the ups and downs they've been through? Yet they're still together. They're successful people. Learn how they did it, so you can grow and obtain wisdom and knowledge and understanding. You've been through some things in the States and you didn't connect with your family in the right way. I'm telling you as a man, you need to sit down with them over a cup of tea. Do you have the guts to do it?"

"Yes."

"And when you're talking with them, if your heart doesn't jump with pride, honour, and astonishment, then you're empty inside 'cause what they've done takes strength. You also need to stay away from party girls and to focus on one woman. What are you gonna do if you meet some chick in a flimsy little outfit, a fishnet dress maybe, and she's five-seven, nicely built, up on heels with plenty of makeup, and she has a bunch of X, and she comes to you, and says, 'Bring your pretty little butt over here, Shauny?' You have to make a choice. She's mesmerizing. She's tantalizing. She's sexy. Her breath smells like cinnamon and jasmine. Her bed is perfumed with myrrh and aloes like the harlot in Proverbs 7. Are you gonna go for the temptation that leads you down the path of destruction?"

"No!" I say, shaking my head.

"Are you gonna allow her perfume and drugs to seduce you, to take you to the demonic realm?"

"Absolutely not. I'm out of that lifestyle.

"Okay. Well don't forget to talk to your parents."

In 2008, I sit down in my parents' dining room, its walls white and the floor wooden. Below a vase of fragrant sunflowers, roses and daisies, the purple table cover from India is embellished with a golden elephant. The French windows are open, allowing a cool breeze carrying the scent of lavender indoors. The view outside is of yellow and purple flowers and green plants circumscribing a paved back yard on which slinks Harry, my parents' ginger cat. In front of an old brown wooden back fence, water is trickling down a series of pots towards a grey Buddha.

"T-Bone suggested I ask you how you've managed to stay together for so long," I say.

"The main thing is having things in common," Mum says. "When you meet someone initially you've got to have physical attraction. But there has to be more than attraction for a relationship to sustain. During the high hormonal phase, which can last up to two years, you don't see the other person's faults. After that, if you don't have things in common, you start to irritate each other."

"Sounds like the story of my life," I say.

"That's been the trouble with your relationships," Mum

says. "You have an initial attraction to these beautiful women that you have absolutely nothing in common with – a couple of whom you couldn't even speak their language."

We laugh.

"As soon as that physical attraction fizzles out, that's it. As well as your interests, you're sharing your life. Me and your dad like hiking, going to the gym and ballroom dancing. It's also important to have things that you do differently to give each other space. I do yoga and your dad doesn't. Because I've studied psychology, I'm familiar with similarity theory. There's a correlation between the more things people have in common and the length of the relationship. Right down to basic things such as age, socio-economic background, education, religion, ethnicity, the area they're born in. Me and your dad are the poster children for that theory. Not that marriages from different backgrounds don't succeed. Plenty do, but the differences add pressure."

"But out of all of the people you went to school with who got married and shared those factors, how many got divorced?" I ask.

"Most of them," Mum says.

"So what additional factors have kept you together?" I ask.

"Loving each other," Mum says, staring affectionately at Dad. "We're still in love."

"How many years have you been in love?" I ask.

"We've been married for 45 years, Mum says. "Over the years, we've been a bit in and out of love because we've had arguments and there's been times when we haven't felt as close."

"What's always brought you back together?" I ask.

"The basic notion that we always want to be together. I can't imagine life without your dad," Mum says in a tender voice, tears forming.

Moved by the depth of feeling being expressed, I well up with emotion. I've always wanted a successful relationship, but never thought to ask my parents about theirs. I regret not instigating this conversation sooner and learning more about the beauty of their successful marriage that's been on my doorstep forever. "How about you dad?" I ask.

"Your mum's already signed up for internet dating," Dad says, making us laugh. "Your mum's said it all really. The important one is liking and loving each other, which we do in spite of irritations that have happened. When people who've been together for a long time are asked, 'What are the secrets of your marriage?' you'll hear the clichés and they're perfectly true. The biggest one of all is working at it. It's like a job. We've worked through a lot of difficult things over the years and it takes effort. A lot of people aren't prepared to put the effort into it."

"As soon as something goes wrong, they're off," Mum says. "Divorce is so much easier now than when we were young. People think at the first stumbling block, *He doesn't love me anymore. I've had enough of this. I've seen someone else that I fancy.* It's too easy. I believe that if you stick with it, you can get over those feelings."

"But what about all of the people in unhappy relationships who stay in them because they don't want to leave their comfort zones?" I say.

"There are lots of marriages in which people dislike each other intensely, but they stay together because of children," Dad says. "Sometimes there's economic reasons why they won't divorce."

"Don't you think they should leave their comfort zones and seek a happier life?" I ask.

"You shouldn't shoot off at the first thing that goes wrong," Mum says. "If you've tried to make the marriage work, then it's okay to move on. I know people in very unhappy marriages who've stayed because they don't want to sell the house and divide their assets. It's an economic thing. A lot of women stay with men for that reason."

"People often resist change," Dad says. "They don't want to look for a house or an apartment when they've got their own chair, TV remote and all that stuff."

"If you're in a really bad relationship, abusive or violent, or you're really unhappy, it's best to move on," Mum says. "You tried really hard with Sumiko, but in the end you had to end it because of the abuse. No one should put up with cruelty, physical or mental."

"So what else keeps you two together?" I ask.

"We think alike," Dad says. "With politics, your mum has a left liberal tendency like I do. We see things in the news and we think alike about the horrible things going on in the world. Your mum has an overriding kindness that I love. When I had my hernia operation, your mum was terrific. She came home from work, was cooking me meals and taking really good care of me. It made me want to be ill a little bit longer. If ever your mum gets ill, which I hope she never does, I'd do the same. It's nice that we can count on that."

"When I was a secretary," Mum says, "I wanted to train to be a teacher. Your dad supported me when I gave up my job to do the teacher training. He helped, did more around the house, cooking and stuff. There were married women at university with me whose husbands really resented the fact that they were going to be educated into higher positions than they were. There were actually marriage breakups and divorces because of the resentment from husbands. They didn't trust their partners and they didn't respect what their partners were trying to achieve. They wanted their wives to be an extension of themselves, not individual people with their own needs and ambitions."

"What about staying together through the hard times?" I ask.

"One of our biggest tests was your imprisonment," Mum says. "When something goes wrong, it either splits you up – the pressure is too much and you can't deal with it, and you blame each other – or it cements you together. There were tensions during your imprisonment, but we dealt with it and it cemented us together. I'm very proud of the fact that we were able to support you and keep the family together. That was the test of our relationship really – when it could have all fallen apart."

In September 2013, I ask my meditation teacher about love.

"It's very easy to get caught in the trap of love that's expressed in popular society," Andrew says. "Hollywood love. The aspirations of the teenager to fall in love. It's a bit like doses of sugar. People pursue it all of their lives without realizing they've been fed the saccharine of false love. They look for it in their relationships. Of course there's a buzz in the beginning of any relationship and you think, *This is wonderful.* But that's not real love. That's the whizz-bang of a new relationship. It expands you," Andrew says in a euphoric tone. "You expand into it. It's good for the ego because it makes you feel wonderful. There's no judgement of your partner because you're expanding at a phenomenal rate – but that can't be maintained. It's like taking a drug. For a short period of time, it's intoxicating. Eventually, you come back down to earth. Then you have to deal with the reality of that person, their faults and the rest of it, their ego and your ego."

"Maybe I went from person to person because love was another drug I was addicted to. I've never lasted longer than three years with anyone. When the intoxication wore off, I went to someone else."

"Love is a conduit that's opened up within you. You think that you're getting it from outside, but it's a mechanism that's opened up within you. You use an external person to turn the tap and the love flows. You think its flowing from the person, but it's a force inside you."

"So how do I nurture that force?" I ask.

"You seek that internal expression of love. You have to identify where it is within you and give it time and attention. For most people, the one person in the world who they find most difficult to love is themselves. You need to distinguish at some point because it's not loving the ego. It's loving the self."

"What's the difference?"

"Ego love confines and limits and importantly, separates you. Genuine love within yourself allows you to expand. You feel as though your love is expanding naturally to all people. When you're sitting and you see a group of people, your sense of love goes to every one of them not just the pretty ones. That's how you tell the distinction: does it make you separate or do you join the rest of humanity?"

"In prison, I studied different theories about the meaning of life," I say. "Love was the one that made the most sense. I woke up this morning thinking I need to ask you: is love the meaning of life?"

"It has to be. The whole purpose of us being here is to join with the universal and give up the selfish aspects of our character. Connecting with the universal is pure love. There are various stages of love you go through. It starts with small children who are selfish because it's in their nature to look after themselves. They are taught to give and be kind to others. Gradually, they learn empathy and consideration. It grows from that to friendships and love of parents. Then you go and find a partner, who you learn to love fully and unconditionally if you are willing to and have the capacity. It doesn't matter what they do to you, your love is unconditional. That doesn't mean allowing them to walk all over you. It's willingness to have unconditional love. When you've achieved that then the next step is to give unconditional love to everyone. Treat everyone as you treat yourself and be of service to humanity. These various levels of love gradually move you towards the concept of universal love."

"That reminds me of the four types of love described by the Ancient Greek philosophers."

"Yes," Andrew says. "The natural affection between parents and offspring is the Greek storge. Philia is the mental affection between friendships, the dispassionate virtuous love described by Aristotle. Éros is physical love. Your desires and longing. That should actually be at the bottom. Agápe is spiritual selfless love, which is at the top."

"Does the ego have its biggest investment in eros?" I ask.

"Sex is the base form of love. It's purely physical. These definitions of love go up in levels. You know because it's a form of expansion. You go from satisfying yourself to satisfying in a relationship, then you have children and you satisfy a family, and then you move from that to society and to servicing humankind. If you think continually about sex, it will fill your subconscious."

"Not thinking continually about sex doesn't come easy for me," I say.

We laugh.

"Especially when I'm falling asleep and waking up," I add.

"That's interesting," Andrew says. "You might actually be using it as a distraction."

"In what way?" I ask.

"We all seek love and intimacy. The ultimate love

and intimacy is joining with the true self, but there are gradations. The base love, eros, is a reflection of a desire for intimacy and connection with the true self. If we lack that intimacy with other human beings, it's going to express itself with a desire for sexual gratification. Once you achieve real intimacy with another human being, and more importantly with yourself, then the sexual desire diminishes."

"Isn't sexual desire diminishing a function of testosterone?" I ask. "I have a transsexual friend in prison who cut one testicle off and then more recently the other. Now I imagine that my friend's unshackled from the sex drive that's such a dominant force in the way men think. I sometimes think what a relief that would be to have that hormone reduced. Instead of day-dreaming about sex, I could get lots more work done."

"Just wait until you get to my age," Andrew says. "I can look back at when I was a young man and think, *What was the issue here?* As you get older, you produce less testosterone."

"How much older?" I ask. "I was like that in my twenties and now I'm 44! When's it going to slow down?"

"It begins to diminish around 50."

"So I shouldn't go and cut them off before 50 then?"

We laugh.

"As it begins to diminish," Andrew says, "I've found it to be less of a burden because it's always been such a distraction."

"A friend just messaged me that he quit drugs," I say. "It was the struggle of his life. Now all he can think about is sex. He asked me if he's replaced one addiction with another."

"Absolutely," Andrew says. "You cannot give up a habit unless you replace it with something else. The perfect habit to replace it with is being in the present. It's subtle and more difficult, but all craving lasts for five minutes. If you can bring yourself into the present moment, you're taking your attention away from the craving. At a drug rehab, I was speaking about being in the present moment, and this chap says to me that drug cravings only last for four or five minutes and then they pass. I told him that if he had the tools to be in the present moment, he could observe that craving and it would reduce significantly. Also, coming into the present has the effect of replacing the craving. I showed him some simple relaxation techniques; for example, focussing his attention on his breath where it enters the body. That allowed him to become present. His attention was on the physical body and away from his craving. After a few minutes, he diminished the craving. He told me that he'd reached the age of 50 and he'd never been taught to do this. He said, 'How can it be that you've just taught us something in half an hour that's so valuable for our rehabilitation?'"

"So he only had to concentrate on his breathing for the length of the craving to stop him going back to drugs?"

"In the beginning," Andrew says. "It takes a month to learn a new habit. If you do the breathing exercise for a month, the craving is replaced. Your chap who's given up drugs and thinks about sex all of the time, now what he has to do is take on something else to replace it."

"But not completely give up sex?" I ask, brows raised.

"No, no, no, no, no," Andrew says. "That wouldn't be fun. There'd be no fulfilment in life. But if something's become an addiction, you must replace it with a healthy habit. It's gradation. From drugs down to sex. From sex down to golf or whatever it is."

"If I ever go from sex down to golf, please kill me," I say, smiling.

"He's got to replace it with something," Andrew says, "and you and I have replaced things with meditation and staying in the present."

Thanks to bad experience and good advice, I no longer get married at the drop of a hat. In the early stages of dating, I assume I'm not the only one putting my best face forward and that most people have skeletons in their closets – but maybe not as big as mine. I tend to gloss over that I'm a workaholic who rarely leaves his computer – a trait that has sent some women running for the hills. No matter how strong the physical attraction, I try to remain vigilant for warning signs in my prospective partner – whether they are drug and alcohol dependencies or plates getting smashed. A few years after my release, I went on an Internet date. After we discussed my prison experience, my date revealed that she had a gun in her attic stashed by her son who'd recently committed a bank robbery. The gun-in-the-attic story would have amused the old me, but needless to say, I didn't go back. It was a road I've already been on and I know how it ends. After bringing the stress of incarceration upon myself, I want to live a relaxed life. I understand there must be give and take, but I'm more careful due to the advice given by Dr. Owen, and thanks to Andrew, I think more deeply about love and its various meanings and applications in relation to my own behaviour.

I'm presently in a long-distance relationship with Callie, a yoga instructor. We met in her class. It wasn't her striking looks, flame-like hair and psychedelic leggings that gave me gooseflesh. It was her beautiful voice. Callie sang a chant at the end that struck a chord in my soul. For months afterwards, we emailed back and forth, discovering things that we like in common such as gangster movies, blueberries, rave DJ's and episodes of *Breaking Bad* and *Prison Break*. So far, she's put up with me without having to raise an iron. Although the hormonal burst-of-passion phase is being prolonged by the distance between us – she lives near Liverpool and I near London – I feel that we're building a solid foundation of love and friendship. She's so relaxing to be around – except for last night when fast asleep I received two punches to the ribs for what she described as me "snoring like a pig being choked." But at least she wasn't armed with a Ginsu knife. I have a feeling that she might save me from my workaholism. Since telling her that I've never been on holiday in my adult life, she's been insisting that we spend a month at an ashram in India – a goal I wrote home excitedly from prison about. We've recently started planning the trip online. By applying what I've learned about love over the years, it seems that I've finally found a good partner.

Lesson 10:
Take Time for Introspection

"Your visions will become clear only when you can look into your own heart. Who looks outside, dreams; who looks inside, awakes."
– Carl Jung

Before my arrest, the word "introspection" means nothing to me, and I couldn't care less to find out. But inside, I'm forced to look within myself for the first time. There's a cloud in my head from years of drug abuse that I don't know exists until it lifts when I sober up behind bars.

All of a sudden, I feel as if I've magically regressed to the clearer-thinking person I was before drugs. The insanity of my behaviour and bad choices are apparent. My introspection begins with a review of my life and the decisions that led to my arrest. I see the shy student I was taking Ecstasy for the first time, foolishly convinced I'm only experimenting and can stop whenever I want. I see my friends in America doing the same and acting crazy, all of us reinforcing each other's behaviour, sliding down the same slope at accelerating speed. I shudder at the thought of the dangerous situations I put myself in. I don't understand how I'm still alive.

The general review of my life is the start of introspection, but it takes meditation to observe my thoughts at work. In a seated position in jail as I try to quieten my mind with my eyes closed, whatever is occupying me the most on a particular day displays on my thought screen. I'm amazed by the relentless barrage of thoughts. I'm perplexed by where they come from. I doubt that they can be stopped, controlled or modulated, but over time there are moments when meditation allows these things. The more I watch my thoughts, the more self-understanding I gain.

The thought journal Dr. Owen tells me to start is a chore at first. But over time, it becomes the most powerful tool I have for self-analysis.

April 11 2006

The person in front of me in the chow hall forgot his orange. The chow server asked me to give it to him. I did, and was accused of trying to steal it. I felt deeply offended but said nothing. The thought simmered throughout the night.

I was told I had three items of mail in the guard tower. I never received it and went to sleep worrying if it had been trashed.

April 12

I sat in Cultural Diversity class suffering social-anxiety symptoms, including worrying if my armpit sweat was visible.

Was happy with my mail and penned a response to a person with whom I have a lot in common.

Extremely loud F-16 fighter jet noises not only triggered fear of them coming through my cell wall, but also a fantasy about dropping from a troubled plane into the ocean. I wondered how I'd hit the water, if and what bones would break, and if I'd be able to swim. Had visions of being eaten alive by sharks.

April 18

Anxiety level up. While at chow someone entered my cell and took my chess set. I'm trying to read but can't help wondering if either someone borrowed it without asking or it was stolen.

Later on, I found the chess set hidden under my mattress. A practical joke. I settled down.

April 23

My thoughts are filled with my dad and sister's imminent visits. I can't wait to see them. We have so much to discuss. The realization that they'll be here soon never fails to bring a smile to my face. So grateful that my family have come so far to see me after everything I've put them through.

Upset about the store not selling peanut butter for two weeks, as all I buy are peanut butter, pretzels and crackers. Feeling hungry, but I remind myself about not being attached to food as described in my yoga books.

April 26

Was chosen to speak in front of two dozen people during Cultural Diversity class, defending a viewpoint about the erosion of civil rights. I somehow managed to get my point across and was applauded. My jitteriness rose, and when it was over, I felt the nerves and nausea I experienced after being in a car crash. Despite these symptoms, I thought, Perhaps I can speak in front of the class after all. Then I told myself, You spoke for less than two minutes. You're crazy if you think you can speak at length without choking up.

May 1

The hostage situation [an inmate has kidnapped a female guard and is holding her at knifepoint] has wiped out my positive thoughts surrounding my dad and sister's visit. I'm worried that the rest of their visits will be cancelled. Disappointed for my dad and sister after travelling so far to see me.

May 2 – 5

Some visits were cancelled and I had to battle for others. Time meant for relaxing with my family was tense. Their disappointment was palpable, which increased my anxiety. Happy to see my dad and sister, but sad about the hostage situation.

May 5

Someone said people were upset because I had some visits whereas today's visits for everyone were cancelled (including mine). Increased my stress.

4:30pm Meditated to reduce stress. Thoughts bubbled up. Hostage situation. Writing. Feel as if I'm in shock from worrying about my dad and sister. Really concerned about my dad who noticed my excessive perspiration at Xmas time; during the final visit he expressed his concern that I may be becoming institutionalized. My dad has had panic attacks since my arrest, and I feel guilt, worsened by his recent concerns. Realize I'll be home next year, and shouldn't be making too big a deal out of things.

May 7

Something I read In Erik Erikson's Identity: Youth and Crisis reminded me of me and made me stop and think for a few minutes. "Many adults feel that their worth as people consists entirely in what they are "going at" in the future and not in what they are in the present. The strain consequently developed in their bodies, which are always "on the go," with the engine racing even at moments of rest, is a powerful contribution to the much discussed psychosomatic diseases of our time."

Wrote for 6½ hours and feel happier. A sense of accomplishment.

By capturing my thoughts on paper, I'm able to look back and identify thought patterns and shifts in emotion. Thanks to the journal, I identify a manic state in which I describe being so euphoric, I feel as if I can walk to the chow hall on my hands. Looking back from a calmer perspective, I seem like a different person. I see how my excitement leads to delusional thinking and my tendency to make mistakes becomes much clearer. I also identify a pattern of worrying about small things.

In The Beano, I say to my meditation teacher, "One of the things I've noticed when I look over my life lessons is that before I got arrested I never stopped to think about the consequences of my actions. I probably wouldn't have learned half of these lessons without introspection. How important is introspection?"

"It comes down to the issue of reason," Andrew says. "You have to reason things out. For example, after meditation, it's good to sit and talk about the things that arise. Either by having a discussion with yourself or another person. It's very important to understand the lessons that are being provided to you. You may want to talk about what your fears are. What is it that arose within a dream or meditation? Should it be something you should fear? How do you go about tackling it? What is it telling you about your character?"

"In prison, I kept a thought journal and a dream journal."

"I think it's very important to keep a journal," Andrew says. "I keep a journal of things that come to me. Stuff is always coming up from the subconscious. Wisdom comes up from the area of universal knowledge. I have to separate the informative from the rubbish. When something positive comes up, it's good to note it, and see how it can be of value to you for your greatest purpose. You can put it towards getting money if you like, but the greatest purpose is spiritual growth. You must ask yourself, *What's the value of this knowledge and information?* You must use your reason to identify and process it. Sometimes I'm reminded of negative experiences from my past that come up from the memory bank, and I think, *Why am I thinking about this now? What's the value of it to me? What must I do in order to process it? Should I send myself positive messages of love to balance it?* I don't care about the experience itself or to relive it. I want to know how I can use the knowledge of it to advance my highest purpose. It's arising for a reason. It means it's now time to process it. Introspection is a very important part of this process."

"I was basically forced into introspection," I say. "I imagine most people don't do it, just like me before my arrest. Why do you think that is the case if introspection is so valuable?"

"Two years ago, I was sitting beside a lake in Switzerland," Andrew says. "When you're sitting beside a lake the light is reflected off the lake. You can't see what's down there. Your subconscious is like that. Generally speaking, people can't see what's in there. What you can't see you're fearful of. The ego does not want you to go down there because beyond the subconscious exists your true self, so the ego creates a fear factor."

"So the barrier to introspection for most people is a self-protection mechanism designed by the ego?" I ask.

"Yes. It's the bogey man under the bed thing. You can't see what's under there, so you fear the worst, depending on how colourful your imagination is. You also know that there is fearful stuff down there and it makes you worry more, so you avoid it. The subconscious is constantly sending messages up. If you keep busy, you don't have to see them. And that's why people don't want to be still or alone."

"I think that's why a lot of prisoners turn to harder drugs in prison. They don't want to be reminded where they are, why they're there, what they did to put themselves there, the hurt their situations are causing their loved ones. They want to escape from all that."

"They do not wish to do the inner work," Andrew says. "It starts with falling still and seeing what comes up. There's a permeable membrane between you and the subconscious level. Stuff passes both ways. If you think continually of money, it will fill your subconscious, and it will express itself in the external world. But it also works the other way. Stuff bubbles up from the subconscious to the conscious level, especially just when you're falling asleep. Why does it happen there? It happens all of the time, but you notice it the most when you're falling asleep because your mind is still. A wise person, being present with a still mind, reads the messages from the subconscious all of the time."

Incarceration forced me to begin monitoring my mental and emotional processes. Dr. Owen gave me some powerful advice for the inner journey and Andrew continues to guide me. If I'd arrived in America with such knowledge, my life would have turned out differently.

Writing this book refocused me on self-examination with an intensity I hadn't employed since incarceration. When asked to ponder the ten most important lessons from my life, I didn't know where to start. Although I knew I'd learned lessons, I hadn't considered aggregating them. In order to structure this book, I sat down with my family and wrote the numbers 1 to 10 on a notepad. We came up with clusters of ideas based on our viewpoints and experiences which I distilled into ten lessons. But as I started to write, the structure of the book took on a life of its own. Things that we prioritized in our brain-storming took a back seat as more important lessons emerged.

When I get enthusiastic about a project, I pour my heart and soul into it. From the get-go, I considered this book an opportunity to help people on a large scale and not something to be taken lightly. During the day, ideas bubbled up from my subconscious when I was least expecting them – such as cooking breakfast – and I would dash to the computer to type them up before I forgot them. Lots of ideas arrived during my morning meditation and when I was falling asleep – times when my brain was less preoccupied with everyday stuff. When editing, I tend to reread and rewrite to the point of fanaticism. For example, the first page of my jail memoir, *Hard Time*, was rewritten over 1000 times. Each time I rewrote a chapter of this book, my memory of the lesson strengthened. Every time I read what Dr. Owen or Andrew said reinforced their lessons, and I sometimes felt as if I were coming to a greater understanding of their wisdom. This project provoked much discussion among my family and friends. In my twenties, I only used to bare my soul to people when I was high on Ecstasy. Having conversations about this book – which necessitated sharing my feelings – has brought me closer to the people I love the most.

Working on this book has been a constant reminder to do right and to continue to expand as a person in the way I've been doing since my release from prison. I hope this book has inspired you, and at the very least, provoked some thought about your own life.

Hard Time 2ⁿᵈ Edition

Chapter 1

Sleep deprived and scanning for danger, I enter a dark cell on the second floor of the maximum-security Madison Street jail in Phoenix, Arizona, where guards and gang members are murdering prisoners. Behind me, the metal door slams heavily. Light slants into the cell through oblong gaps in the door, illuminating a prisoner cocooned in a white sheet, snoring lightly on the top bunk about two thirds of the way up the back wall. Relieved there is no immediate threat, I place my mattress on the grimy floor. Desperate to rest, I notice movement on the cement-block walls. *Am I hallucinating?* I blink several times. The walls appear to ripple. Stepping closer, I see the walls are alive with insects. I flinch. So many are swarming, I wonder if they're a colony of ants on the move. To get a better look, I put my eyes right up to them. They are mostly the size of almonds and have antennae. American cockroaches. I've seen them in the holding cells downstairs in smaller numbers, but nothing like this. A chill spreads over my body. I back away.

Something alive falls from the ceiling and bounces off the base of my neck. I jump. With my night vision improving, I spot cockroaches weaving in and out of the base of the fluorescent strip light. Every so often one drops onto the concrete and resumes crawling. Examining the bottom bunk, I realise why my cellmate is sleeping at a higher elevation: cockroaches are pouring from gaps in the decrepit wall at the level of my bunk. The area is thick with them. Placing my mattress on the bottom bunk scatters them. I walk towards the toilet, crunching a few under my shower sandals. I urinate and grab the toilet roll. A cockroach darts from the centre of the roll onto my hand, tickling my fingers. My arm jerks as if it has a mind of its own, losing the cockroach and the toilet roll. Using a towel, I wipe the bulk of them off the bottom bunk, stopping only to shake the odd one off my hand. I unroll my mattress. They begin to regroup and inhabit my mattress. My adrenaline is pumping so much, I lose my fatigue.

Nauseated, I sit on a tiny metal stool bolted to the wall. *How will I sleep? How's my cellmate sleeping through the infestation and my arrival?* Copying his technique, I cocoon myself in a sheet and lie down, crushing more cockroaches. The only way they can access me now is through the breathing hole I've left in the sheet by the lower half of my face. Inhaling their strange musty odour, I close my eyes. I can't sleep. I feel them crawling on the sheet around my feet. *Am I imagining things?* Frightened of them infiltrating my breathing hole, I keep opening my eyes. Cramps cause me to rotate onto my other side. Facing the wall, I'm repulsed by so many of them just inches away. I return to my original side.

The sheet traps the heat of the Sonoran Desert to my

body, soaking me in sweat. Sweat tickles my body, tricking my mind into thinking the cockroaches are infiltrating and crawling on me. The trapped heat aggravates my bleeding skin infections and bedsores. I want to scratch myself, but I know better. The outer layers of my skin have turned soggy from sweating constantly in this concrete oven. Squirming on the bunk fails to stop the relentless itchiness of my skin. Eventually, I scratch myself. Clumps of moist skin detach under my nails. Every now and then I become so uncomfortable, I have to open my cocoon to waft the heat out, which allows the cockroaches in. It takes hours to drift to sleep. I only manage a few hours. I awake stuck to the soaked sheet, disgusted by the cockroach carcasses compressed against the mattress.

The cockroaches plague my new home until dawn appears at the dots in the metal grid over a begrimed strip of four-inch-thick bullet-proof glass at the top of the back wall – the cell's only source of outdoor light. They disappear into the cracks in the walls, like vampire mist retreating from sunlight. But not all of them. There were so many on the night shift that even their vastly reduced number is too many to dispose of. And they act like they know it. They roam around my feet with attitude, as if to make it clear that I'm trespassing on their turf.

My next set of challenges will arise not from the insect world, but from my neighbours. I'm the new arrival, subject to scrutiny about my charges just like when I'd run into the Aryan Brotherhood prison gang on my first day at the medium-security Towers jail a year ago. I wish my cellmate would wake up, brief me on the mood of the locals and introduce me to the head of the white gang. No such luck. Chow is announced over a speaker system in a crackly robotic voice, but he doesn't stir.

I emerge into the day room for breakfast. Prisoners in

black-and-white bee-striped uniforms gather under the metal-grid stairs and tip dead cockroaches into a trash bin from plastic peanut-butter containers they'd set as traps during the night. All eyes are on me in the chow line. Watching who sits where, I hold my head up, put on a solid stare and pretend to be as at home in this environment as the cockroaches. It's all an act. I'm lonely and afraid. I loathe having to explain myself to the head of the white race, who I assume is the toughest murderer. I've been in jail long enough to know that taking my breakfast to my cell will imply that I have something to hide.

The gang punishes criminals with certain charges. The most serious are sex offenders, who are KOS: Kill On Sight. Other charges are punishable by SOS – Smash On Sight – such as drive-by shootings because women and kids sometimes get killed. It's called convict justice. Gang members are constantly looking for people to beat up because that's how they earn their reputations and tattoos. The most serious acts of violence earn the highest-ranking tattoos. To be a full gang member requires murder. I've observed the body language and techniques inmates trying to integrate employ. An inmate with a spring in his step and an air of confidence is likely to be accepted. A person who avoids eye contact and fails to introduce himself to the gang is likely to be preyed on. Some of the failed attempts I saw ended up with heads getting cracked against toilets, a sound I've grown familiar with. I've seen prisoners being extracted on stretchers who looked dead – one had yellow fluid leaking from his head. The constant violence gives me nightmares, but the reality is that I put myself in here, so I force myself to accept it as a part of my punishment.

It's time to apply my knowledge. With a self-assured stride, I take my breakfast bag to the table of white inmates covered in neo-Nazi tattoos, allowing them to question me.

"Mind if I sit with you guys?" I ask, glad exhaustion has deepened my voice.

"These seats are taken. But you can stand at the corner of the table."

The man who answered is probably the head of the gang. I size him up. Cropped brown hair. A dangerous glint in Nordic-blue eyes. Tiny pupils that suggest he's on heroin. Weightlifter-type veins bulging from a sturdy neck. Political ink on arms crisscrossed with scars. About the same age as me, thirty-three.

"Thanks. I'm Shaun from England." I volunteer my origin to show I'm different from them but not in a way that might get me smashed.

"I'm Bullet, the head of the whites." He offers me his fist to bump. "Where you roll in from, wood?"

Addressing me as wood is a good sign. It's what white gang members on a friendly basis call each other.

"Towers jail. They increased my bond and re-classified me to maximum security."

"What's your bond at?"

"I've got two $750,000 bonds," I say in a monotone. This is no place to brag about bonds.

"How many people you kill, brother?" His eyes drill into mine, checking whether my body language supports my story. My body language so far is spot on.

"None. I threw rave parties. They got us talking about drugs on wiretaps." Discussing drugs on the phone does not warrant a $1.5 million bond. I know and beat him to his next question. "Here's my charges." I show him my charge sheet, which includes conspiracy and leading a crime syndicate – both from running an Ecstasy ring.

Bullet snatches the paper and scrutinises it. Attempting to pre-empt his verdict, the other whites study his face. On edge, I wait for him to respond. Whatever he says next will determine whether I'll be accepted or victimised…

My Social-Media Links

Email: attwood.shaun@hotmail.co.uk
Blog: Jon's Jail Journal
Website: shaunattwood.com
Twitter: @shaunattwood
YouTube: Shaun Attwood
LinkedIn: Shaun Attwood
Goodreads: Shaun Attwood
Facebook pages: Shaun Attwood, Jon's Jail Journal,
T-Bone Appreciation Society

I welcome feedback on any of my books.
Thank you for the Amazon reviews!

Shaun's Books

English Shaun Trilogy
Party Time
Hard Time
Prison Time

War on Drugs Series
Pablo Escobar: Beyond Narcos
American Made: Who Killed Barry Seal?
Pablo Escobar or George HW Bush
The Cali Cartel: Beyond Narcos
We Are Being Lied To: The War on Drugs (Expected 2019)
The War Against Weed (Expected 2019)

Un-Making a Murderer:
The Framing of Steven Avery and Brendan Dassey
The Mafia Philosopher: Two Tonys
Life Lessons

Pablo Escobar's Story (Expected 2018)
T-Bone (Expected 2022)

Hard Time

As a teenager in an industrial UK town, Shaun Attwood covets the American Dream. He moves to Arizona with only student credit cards and becomes a millionaire. After throwing Ecstasy parties for thousands of ravers, Shaun bumps heads with Sammy the Bull Gravano, an Italian Mafia mass murderer, who puts a hit out on him.

The dream turns into a nightmare when a SWAT team smashes Shaun's door down. Inside Arizona's deadliest jail, Shaun struggles to survive against an unpredictable backdrop of gang violence and sickening human-rights violations. Over time and bolstered by the love and support of his fiancée and family, he uses incarceration for learning and introspection.

With a tiny pencil sharpened on a cell door, Shaun documents the conditions: dead rats in the food, cockroaches crawling in his ears at night, murders and riots… Smuggled out of maximum-security and posted online, his writing shines the international media spotlight on the plight of the prisoners in Sheriff Joe Arpaio's jail.

Join best-selling author Shaun Attwood on a harrowing voyage into the darkest recesses of human existence in *Hard Time*, the second book from the English Shaun trilogy.

Party Time

In *Party Time*, Shaun Attwood arrives in Phoenix, Arizona a penniless business graduate from a small industrial town in England. Within a decade, he becomes a stock-market millionaire.

But he is leading a double life.

After taking his first Ecstasy pill at a rave in Manchester as a shy student, Shaun becomes intoxicated by the party lifestyle that changes his fortune. Making it his personal mission to bring the English rave scene to the Arizona desert, Shaun becomes submerged in a criminal underworld, throwing parties for thousands of ravers and running an Ecstasy ring in competition with the Mafia mass murderer "Sammy The Bull" Gravano.

As greed and excess tear through his life, Shaun experiences eye-watering encounters with Mafia hit men and crystal-meth addicts, extravagant debaucheries with superstar DJs and glitter girls, and ingests enough drugs to kill a herd of elephants. This is his story.

Prison Time

Sentenced to 9½ years in Arizona's state prison for distributing Ecstasy, Shaun finds himself living among gang members, sexual predators and drug-crazed psychopaths. After being attacked by a Californian biker in for stabbing a girlfriend, Shaun writes about the prisoners who befriend, protect and inspire him. They include T-Bone, a massive African American ex-Marine who risks his life saving vulnerable inmates from rape, and Two Tonys, an old-school Mafia murderer who left the corpses of his rivals from Arizona to Alaska. They teach Shaun how to turn incarceration to his advantage, and to learn from his mistakes.

Shaun is no stranger to love and lust in the heterosexual world, but the tables are turned on him inside. Sexual advances come at him from all directions, some cleverly disguised, others more sinister – making Shaun question his sexual identity.

Resigned to living alongside violent, mentally-ill and drug-addicted inmates, Shaun immerses himself in psychology and philosophy to try to make sense of his past behaviour, and begins applying what he learns as he adapts to prison life. Encouraged by Two Tonys to explore fiction as well, Shaun reads over 1000 books which, with support from a brilliant psychotherapist, Dr Owen, speed along his personal development. As his ability to deflect daily threats improves, Shaun begins to look forward to his release with optimism and a new love waiting for him. Yet the words of Aristotle from one of Shaun's books will prove prophetic: "We cannot learn without pain."

About Shaun Attwood

Shaun Attwood is a former stock-market millionaire and Ecstasy supplier turned public speaker, author and activist, who is banned from America for life. His story was featured worldwide on National Geographic Channel as an episode of Locked Up/Banged Up Abroad called Raving Arizona (available on YouTube).

Shaun's writing – smuggled out of the jail with the highest death rate in America run by Sheriff Joe Arpaio – attracted international media attention to the human rights violations: murders by guards and gang members, dead rats in the food, cockroach infestations…

While incarcerated, Shaun was forced to reappraise his life. He read over 1000 books in just under six years. By studying original texts in psychology and philosophy, he sought to better understand himself and his past behaviour. He credits books as being the lifeblood of his rehabilitation.

Shaun tells his story to schools to put young people off drugs and crime. He campaigns against injustice via his books and blog, Jon's Jail Journal. He has appeared on the BBC, Sky News and TV worldwide to talk about issues affecting prisoners' rights. In 2014, Shaun became the patron of Oakleaf, a mental-health charity in Guildford, Surrey, and he announced that all of the proceeds from his book sales are going to charity by way of giving free books to prisoners, prison charities and students in state schools.

Lightning Source UK Ltd.
Milton Keynes UK
UKHW022151211118
332759UK00019B/2052/P

9 781912 885022